IBM Cognos BI v10.2 Administration Essentials

Explore the power and scalability of IBM Cognos BI to achieve effective performance management

Khalid Mehmood Awan

[PACKT] enterprise 🞛
PUBLISHING
professional expertise distilled

BIRMINGHAM - MUMBAI

IBM Cognos BI v10.2 Administration Essentials

First published: January 2014

Production Reference: 2170114

Published by Packt Publishing Ltd.
Livery Place
35 Livery Street
Birmingham B3 2PB, UK.

ISBN 978-1-78217-178-2

www.packtpub.com

Cover Image by Siddhart Ravishankar (sidd.ravishankar@gmail.com)

Credits

Author
Khalid Mehmood Awan

Reviewers
Terry Curran
Manikandan Subbiah
Will Thrash

Acquisition Editor
Vinay Argekar

Comissioning Editor
Mohammed Fahad

Technical Editors
Vrinda Nitesh Bhosale
Pooja Nair
Harshad Vairat

Copy Editors
Sarang Chari
Karuna Narayanan
Shambhavi Pai

Project Coordinator
Sageer Parkar

Proofreader
Ameesha Green

Indexers
Monica Ajmera Mehta
Priya Subramani

Graphics
Yuvraj Mannari

Production Coordinator
Nitesh Thakur

Cover Work
Nitesh Thakur

About the Author

Khalid Mehmood Awan received a Bachelor's degree in Computer Science from the Barani Institute of Information Technology (a joint venture between ROSE and the University of Arid Agriculture, Rawalpindi). In the course of the degree, he stood third in the overall software projects development. The project was a Logic-based Argument Solver developed in LisP (List Programming, an allegro tool).

He is currently working at Mobilink, Pakistan, as a Senior Engineer (Planning) for Mobile Financial Services. He looks after the system KPIs and capacity planning along with product development. In the same organization previously, he was an application engineer and system administrator in the Performance Analysis team. He also worked as a system administrator for the Network Operation Center (NOC) in the same organization. He also has experience in project management working at Mobilink. He has Oracle Financial's Enterprise Resource Planning (ERP) expertise and gained this experience while at Mobilink. This was his first assignment at Mobilink, on which he started working in 2005.

His professional interests focus on system administration, programming, and database administration, and his current projects include MobiCash (a brand name for the Mobile Financial Service of Mobilink). In addition, he also has interests in iOS programming.

Previously, he was a visiting faculty at two local institutes, for teaching Computer Graphics (C Programming and OpenGL with Visual C++). The author joined Artologics (a local software house) and worked in PHP with MySQL as well.

I would like to thank the PAT team as I gathered the images used in the book from their test environment. A list of friends who helped me include MNA bhai, Gill Sb, Naeem, Atif Mughal, Adil, Mobeen Malik, Kaas Sb, Ali, Imran, Saad, Zia, Nowsherwan, and last but not least, Saira.

About the Reviewers

Terry Curran gained an interest in computers while studying for his first degree in Biological Chemistry at the University of Kent. He went on to work as a computer operator for a national supermarket company.

After several years working as a computer operator, he went to Brighton Polytechnic, leaving with a Higher National Diploma in Computer Studies. Upon completion of his studies, he worked as a computer advisor at the City of London Polytechnic, assisting staff and students with their computer problems and providing support for the various database systems in use across the Polytechnic. After taking voluntary redundancy from this post, he proceeded to the University of Stirling where he gained an M.Sc. degree in Software Engineering.

After graduating from the University of Stirling, he commenced working for a software consultancy company. While working for this company, he assisted with the writing of a software package for the publishing industry using Cognos PowerHouse. While there, he gained experience in Business Intelligence reporting tools after being asked to familiarize himself with Cognos Impromptu and PowerPlay in order to promote the use of these tools to clients.

After this company ceased trading, he embarked on a career as a freelance computer consultant and contractor using his experience with Cognos PowerHouse, various computer systems and databases, Cognos Impromptu and PowerPlay, and later Cognos 8 and Cognos 10.

He continues to work as a freelance Cognos Business Intelligence consultant and contractor, making use of his extensive knowledge and experience of IBM Cognos Business Intelligence Reporting. Over the past 15 years, he has worked for a range of industries, including aviation, pharmaceuticals, insurance, and logistics, to name a few.

He is currently working for Ultra Electronics Command and Control Systems as a freelance Cognos consultant.

He was a technical reviewer for the book by *Abhishek Sanghani, IBM Cognos 8 Report Studio Cookbook*, for *Packt Publishing*.

He is the author of *IBM Cognos 10 Framework Manager*, for *Packt Publishing*.

Manikandan Subbiah is an information technology and management leader with over 18 years of well-rounded hands-on global expertise in various business domains and industries, primarily in banking and financial services. He has worked on a variety of technology stacks and open source technologies to solve various challenging problems. He has been a part of various IT solutions that were awarded by international forums. He is passionate about infrastructure solutions, SOA, cloud computing, and mobile applications. He currently works as a Principal Architect for Capgemini UK plc. In his free time, he enjoys travelling, trekking, playing chess, and watching cricket matches.

Will Thrash has over 15 years of experience in data warehousing and Big Data, primarily with IBM Cognos Business Analytics and Microsoft SQL Server, among other platforms. He has worked on data warehouse architecture, database design, cube design, ETL development, training, report writing, and dashboard creation. He also was the CIO of a global manufacturing company and has an MBA from the Wharton School of Business at the University of Pennsylvania.

His current practice is consulting in big data and data warehousing with Market Street Solutions.

I would like to thank my wife, Jill, for the inspiration, and for enduring the time I spend writing and working.

www.PacktPub.com

Support files, eBooks, discount offers and more

You might want to visit www.PacktPub.com for support files and downloads related to your book.

Did you know that Packt offers eBook versions of every book published, with PDF and ePub files available? You can upgrade to the eBook version at www.PacktPub.com and as a print book customer, you are entitled to a discount on the eBook copy. Get in touch with us at service@packtpub.com for more details.

At www.PacktPub.com, you can also read a collection of free technical articles, sign up for a range of free newsletters and receive exclusive discounts and offers on Packt books and eBooks.

http://PacktLib.PacktPub.com

Do you need instant solutions to your IT questions? PacktLib is Packt's online digital book library. Here, you can access, read and search across Packt's entire library of books.

Why Subscribe?

- Fully searchable across every book published by Packt
- Copy and paste, print and bookmark content
- On demand and accessible via web browser

Free Access for Packt account holders

If you have an account with Packt at www.PacktPub.com, you can use this to access PacktLib today and view nine entirely free books. Simply use your login credentials for immediate access.

Instant Updates on New Packt Books

Get notified! Find out when new books are published by following @PacktEnterprise on Twitter, or the *Packt Enterprise* Facebook page.

Table of Contents

Preface

IBM Cognos Business Intelligence (BI) is a web-oriented solution with a variety of available dashboards, analysis tools, reports, events, and many other features. Cognos gives diverse options to users, whether they are data modelers, report authors, analysis teams, administrators, or end users. Cognos works best on RDBMS and OLAP databases that are designed based on warehousing architecture, although it can work with any database design. With the help of Cognos, organizations can use all their company data sources to make better future decisions to help them achieve their goals.

This book is a guide for beginners who are planning to select IBM Cognos BI Administration as their future. This book will help them to grasp the basic knowledge of IBM Cognos BI Administration quickly. The core topics of IBM Cognos BI Administration have been covered in this book, including the architecture of Cognos, its components, configurations, security, and backups. This book will help you to learn the administration tasks necessary for a Cognos environment.

What this book covers

Chapter 1, Introduction to Cognos BI 10.2, will cover an introduction to Cognos and its history along with the new features of Version 10.2. Cognos Administration will also be introduced briefly here.

Chapter 2, The IBM Cognos Configuration Window in Detail, will cover the Cognos Configuration window along with some global configurations.

Chapter 3, Managing IBM Cognos BI Server Components, will cover Cognos BI's components and architecture. The load balancing option will also be discussed at the end of this chapter.

Chapter 4, *Administration Portal*, will cover the Administration Portal in detail, showing you a detailed description for all tabs (including Status, Security, Configuration, and Index Search tabs).

Chapter 5, *Securing IBM Cognos BI*, will cover major security features of Cognos BI, including security architecture, managing authentication providers, overcoming initial security, permissions management, secure features, functionalities and capabilities, Cognos firewall and logging, and Single Sign-on (SSO).

Chapter 6, *Drill-through Definitions*, will cover drill-through definitions, including an overview of them, and some ways to create a drill-through feature/definition.

Chapter 7, *Logging, Auditing, and Cognos Backups*, will cover Cognos BI logging and backups.

Chapter 8, *Additional Configuration and Customization*, will cover the customization of Cognos BI's appearance and functionality, the administration of portlets, and managing user profiles.

Chapter 9, *Administration of New and Enhanced Features*, will cover Cognos Mobile and multiple-tenant environments.

What you need for this book

There is an online resource that covers all the requirements for Cognos BI 10.2's installation. Since only one operating system can be selected at a time while considering installation of Cognos BI, the remaining requirements and prerequisites depend on the OS selected. Hence, to make combinations and see for supported environments and applications, the following link must be visited prior to purchasing Cognos BI and of course, prior to the installation and configuration activity:

```
http://publib.boulder.ibm.com/infocenter/prodguid/v1r0/clarity-
reports/report/html/softwareReqsForProduct?deliverableId=128326274919
3&osPlatform=Linux#
```

Who this book is for

This book is for beginners planning to learn IBM Cognos BI Administration 10.

It is recommended that you have prior basic knowledge of Business Intelligence, systems administration, IBM Cognos BI, databases, and Linux (any flavor).

Conventions

In this book, you will find a number of styles of text that distinguish between different kinds of information. Here are some examples of these styles, and an explanation of their meaning.

New terms and **important words** are shown in bold. Words that you see on the screen, in menus or dialog boxes for example, appear in the text like this: "Right-click on the NE_Name column of the source report in the page view and go to the **Drill-Through Definitions 1** option".

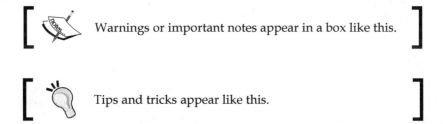

Warnings or important notes appear in a box like this.

Tips and tricks appear like this.

Reader feedback

Feedback from our readers is always welcome. Let us know what you think about this book—what you liked or may have disliked. Reader feedback is important for us to develop titles that you really get the most out of.

To send us general feedback, simply send an e-mail to feedback@packtpub.com, and mention the book title via the subject of your message.

If there is a topic that you have expertise in and you are interested in either writing or contributing to a book, see our author guide on www.packtpub.com/authors.

Customer support

Now that you are the proud owner of a Packt book, we have a number of things to help you to get the most from your purchase.

Errata

Although we have taken every care to ensure the accuracy of our content, mistakes do happen. If you find a mistake in one of our books—maybe a mistake in the text or the code—we would be grateful if you would report this to us. By doing so, you can save other readers from frustration and help us improve subsequent versions of this book. If you find any errata, please report them by visiting http://www.packtpub.com/submit-errata, selecting your book, clicking on the **errata submission form** link, and entering the details of your errata. Once your errata are verified, your submission will be accepted and the errata will be uploaded on our website, or added to any list of existing errata, under the Errata section of that title. Any existing errata can be viewed by selecting your title from http://www.packtpub.com/support.

Piracy

Piracy of copyright material on the Internet is an ongoing problem across all media. At Packt, we take the protection of our copyright and licenses very seriously. If you come across any illegal copies of our works, in any form, on the Internet, please provide us with the location address or website name immediately so that we can pursue a remedy.

Please contact us at copyright@packtpub.com with a link to the suspected pirated material.

We appreciate your help in protecting our authors, and our ability to bring you valuable content.

Questions

You can contact us at questions@packtpub.com if you are having a problem with any aspect of the book, and we will do our best to address it.

1
Introduction to Cognos BI 10.2

IBM Cognos Business Intelligence (BI) is a web-oriented solution with a variety of dashboards, analyses, reports, events, and many other features. Cognos gives diverse options to users whether they are data modelers, report authors, analysis team, administrators, or end users. Cognos works best on an RDBMS and OLAP database that is designed on warehousing architecture, although it can work with any database design. With the help of Cognos, organizations use all their company data sources for better future decisions and can thus achieve their goals.

History of Cognos

Since this book will be focusing more on Cognos Administration, we will not go into its detailed history, but a brief history is necessary for a new audience.

Cognos (Cognos Inc.) started in Ottawa, and they specialized in making Business Intelligence and Performance Management software.

Alan Rushforth founded Cognos in 1969 along with *Peter Glenister*. Later in 1972, *Michael Potter* also joined in.

Cognos Inc. launched their BI 8 product in the year 2005. It included many of the past features of various Cognos Inc. products. Amongst those products were ReportNet, PowerPlay, NoticeCast, DecisionStream, and Cognos 8 Metrics Manager.

Cognos BI 8 also had Express and Extended versions.

The features of Cognos BI 8 include the following:

- **Report Studio**: This is used for creating professional reports.
- **Query Studio**: This is used for ad-hoc reporting.
- **Analysis Studio**: This is used for working in multidimensional cube data.
- **Metric Studio**: This is used for analyzing, monitoring, and reporting on KPIs.
- **Metric Designer**: This is used for defining, loading, and maintaining metrics in Metric Studio.
- **Event Studio**: This helps in notifying decision makers on action-based agents as and when the events happen.
- **Framework Manager**: This is a modeling tool and a semantic metadata-layer software tool, which is used for creating models and packages.
- **PowerPlay Studio**: This was formerly known as PowerPlay Web. This is used to create and view PowerCube data source based reports.
- **Analytic Applications**: This is built on a platform that is adaptable and extensible to Business Analytics (BA). This is also a packaged BI application.

As far as achievements are concerned, IBM Cognos 8 BI won many prizes and awards, including the eWEEK Excellence Award in Analytics and Reportingand Lotus Advisor Editor's Choice Award. The SearchCRM website by TechTarget declared Cognos 8 BI as the Product of the Year in 2005.

IBM acquired Cognos for $4.9 billion in November 2007. Cognos operated as a subsidiary of IBM. In the same year, as per the Maclean's magazine, Cognos to appeared in the Top 100 Employers list in Canada.

Cognos BI became the IBM InfoSphere product line in January 2009 under the IBM Information Management Software brand.

In September 2009, IBM launched Cognos Express. It was started with the purpose of meeting the needs of middle-sized companies, and is an integrated BI and planning solution.

The features of the Express version are as follows:

- **Cognos Express Reporter**: This is used for ad hoc query and self-service reporting
- **Cognos Express Advisor**: This is used for visualization and freeform analysis
- **Cognos Express Xcelerator**: This is a TM1-based business analysis and planning feature with Microsoft Excel and Web interfaces

Prior to the BI offerings, Cognos also offered several Application Development tools:

- IBM Cognos PowerHouse 4GL
- IBM Cognos PowerHouse Web
- IBM Cognos Axiant 4GL

PowerHouse is actually how Cognos made its money before the BI market appeared.

In October 2010, Cognos Version 10 was announced. This was considered a major upgrade to IBM Cognos 8. There were quite a lot of enhancements and new features in this version. Analytics for business users and social collaboration were brought together to achieve real-time BI in a user-friendly environment with all the required features under one roof. Additionally, Cognos Mobile gave users the opportunity to access analysis results and reports on the go, that is, on mobiles such as iPhone, BlackBerry, and iPad.

Now this software is known as IBM Cognos Business Intelligence and Financial Performance Management.

[Historic information was gathered from the IBM website.]

What's new in IBM Cognos BI 10.2

Since administration is involved in every section of an application suite, we will briefly discuss all the new features that appear in Cognos BI Version 10.2.

- Cognos Business Insight has been renamed as IBM Cognos Workspace and Cognos Business Insight Advanced has been renamed as Cognos Workspace Advanced.

- To improve the UI experience, Cognos Workspace (formerly known as Cognos Business Insight) has received new enhancements with tabbed workspaces, a global area in tabbed workspaces, automatic chart recommendations, chart interactions (for example, filter), freezing columns and row headings, viewing column and row heading details, and printing a workspace.

- For a better user experience, a few enhancements have also been made to Cognos Workspace Advanced. This includes enhanced crosstab headers, automatic grouping and summaries for lists, and copying data with number formatting.

- Report Studio has quite a few enhancements including interactive repeater tables, the ability to write query macros in the expression editor, inherited table styles (lists and crosstabs), improved Cognos active report integration with Cognos Workspace, global classes for accessible reports, and prompt API.

- The Cognos Mobile section has been enhanced with two new features that are push notifications for Apple iOS devices and burst reports for Cognos Mobile.

- Now, the **My Folders** area is also accessible to Cognos Lifecycle Manager in addition to the previously available public folders. Secondly, the ability to delete Lifecycle Manager projects is also available now.

- The IBM Cognos search has improved. Users may search up to the field level.

Introduction to Cognos Administration

This book is intended for the new audience that has little knowledge of Business Intelligence, is familiar with system administration, and plans to learn more about IBM Cognos BI Administration. The IBM Cognos Administration section includes the components needed to administer the IBM Cognos software.

The software manual is included in the setup media, whereas product information and knowledge base are available at the IBM Cognos official website, http://pic.dhe.ibm.com/infocenter/cbi/v10r2m0/index.jsp.

IBM Cognos Administration helps to perform the following tasks once the Cognos software has been installed:

- Security management
- Content administration
- Activities and jobs management
- Server administration
- Portal services administration
- Scheduling and task automation
- Monitoring Cognos and working with system KPIs
- Setting up resources such as shared paths, printers, and fonts
- Additional customizations (if required)

The chapters that follow will cover the IBM Cognos Administration capabilities in detail.

Summary

This chapter discussed Cognos BI in general along with its history and some new features in Version 10.2. It also gave an idea of the capabilities of IBM Cognos Administration.

In the next chapter, we will discuss IBM Configuration window in detail. Once installation of Cognos BI has been performed, the next step is to configure it as per our requirements.

2
The IBM Cognos Configuration Window in Detail

In this chapter we will discuss IBM Cognos configurations in detail. This will also familiarize administrators with the IBM Cognos Configuration window. The administration team will be the only team accessing this window. End users (consumers, authors, analysis users, or query users) are never allowed to access Cognos configurations due to security reasons. Using the Configuration window, administrators can add new namespaces (objects). By the end of this chapter, a power user (administrator) will be able to perform all configurations related to the configurations window that includes, but is not limited to, editing services, logging, security authentication providers, cryptographic features, content manager data stores, and so on.

The major topics to be covered in this chapter are:

- Explaining the Cognos Configuration window
- Global configurations

The Cognos Configuration window

The IBM Cognos BI Configuration window requires Java to be configured before it is started. By now you have already configured Java since the Cognos setup requires Java to be installed. Once all required components have been selected and installed, the next step is to configure Cognos BI to either run all components on a single machine, or on multiple machines in the case of distributed installation.

To open the Cognos Configuration window, log in as the Cognos user or the user with which Cognos BI was installed. After logging in, open a terminal session, navigate to the directory, and execute the command as shown in the following screenshot:

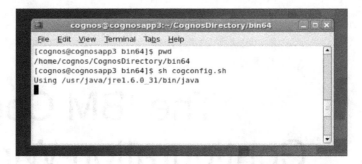

This will open the Cognos BI Configuration window, a part of which is shown in following screenshot, where major configurations can be done. We will discuss each of them later in this chapter. Certain configurations have already been discussed earlier in the book. As you can see, all the configurations have been divided into three major sections: **Environment**, **Security**, and **Data Access**. We shall start with **Environment** first.

The Configurations window has four major sections/areas: the explorer pane, the details pane, the description pane, and the menu along with a toolbar containing some basic icons bound towards actions.

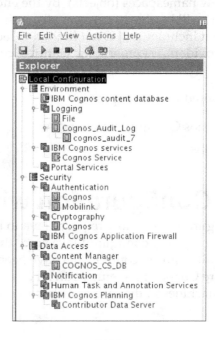

Environment

Once we click on **Environment**, all the related options are shown in the details pane on the right-hand side. If any option on the right-hand side is clicked, its detailed description is displayed in the bottom pane. The following screenshot shows environment-related options. Each of these options may be carefully set depending on the type of installation (single or distributed). In case some component (an application tier, a gateway, or a content manager) was not installed, its options will not be available in this window. Mentioning port numbers in URIs of the Configuration window is mandatory, even if it's a default port; for example, 80 or 1521 in the case of the Oracle database connectivity configuration. Once any option is changed from the default value to a custom value, a yellow icon will indicate the change, and the option may also be reverted to the default value with the same icon shown in the toolbar.

The fields that are mandatory are marked with an orange asterisk sign in the following screenshot:

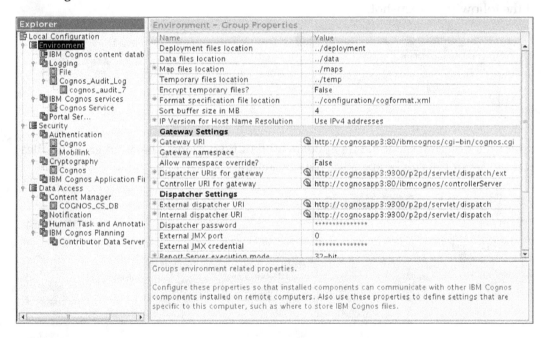

Most of the options available in the Cognos Configuration window can be tested before starting a Cognos service, such as Cognos service itself, the authentication provider, the content manager, and the notification service; hence, this is a great feature to have.

Cognos BI also comes with a built-in content store option if a separate content store (to SQL Server, Oracle, DB2 and so on) is not required. The following screenshot shows the options for the **IBM Cognos content database**.

This option appears if the **IBM Cognos content database** was selected during installation.

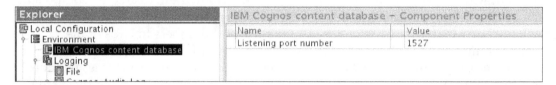

Logging is a key feature that helps in troubleshooting, auditing, and monitoring system performance. Most of the logging-related options are available in the Configuration window. The general options that apply to all logging sections (**File, Database, Event Log**, and so on) can be seen in on the right-hand side of the following screenshot:

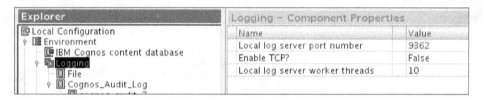

Under the **Logging** section, **File** appears with more options. The number of full files that can be stored can be specified here by setting the size of each file.

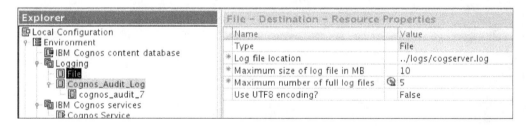

In order to audit the reports, user sessions, jobs, and login history and monitor many other sections of Cognos BI in terms of usage, trend, history, performance. **Logging** is extended to a relational database (for example, Oracle). After adding a logging namespace and enabling an appropriate logging level, for example, basic, request or debug, the database starts to populate with logging- and audit-related data. An audit package (available in the Cognos `Samples` folder) may be published to the Cognos connection. The `Samples` folder is located at `c10_location\webcontent\`.

It also contains some very useful built-in reports. These reports help administrators to monitor and troubleshoot the Cognos **Environment** node. They also help in capacity planning. The following screenshot shows the audit logging namespace and its detailed option:

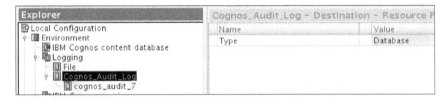

Let us assume that we have selected an Oracle database as our **RDBMS (Relational Database Management System)** for saving audit logs.

The following screenshot displays detailed configuration-related options for an **Oracle database**. These options are almost similar to the content store database configuration options (provided it is an Oracle database).

The basic steps to configure Cognos audit logging include configuring the audit database, setting up the logging levels in the administration portal, and deploying the audit package and audit reports. The audit package and audit reports are available in the Cognos `Samples` folder.

The next main entry under the Cognos **Environment** node is **IBM Cognos services**. When it is clicked on, all the Cognos-related services, which this IBM Cognos server has, appear along with their status. Any service may be disabled or enabled from this window's detailed section. By default, the **IBM Cognos service** section has a **Cognos Service** of the type **Tomcat**. The following screenshot shows the available options for **Cognos Service**. Depending on the available system memory, the memory for **Cognos Service** may be configured in MBs.

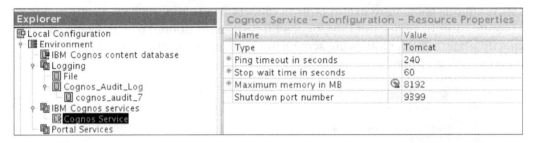

It is possible to deliver the IBM Cognos contents using another portal by configuring **Portal Services**. The following screenshot shows more options related to **Portal Services**:

Security

The second main section in the **Explorer** pane is **Security**, which covers
Authentication, Cryptography, and **IBM Cognos Application Firewall**. Each section
has detailed options available. Considering the general options for **Authentication**,
Cognos BI has certain options that apply to all the security authentication providers.
The following screenshot explains all these options:

Each one of these options plays a vital role towards security. For example, restricting
access to the members of the **Security** namespaces option will allow only users from
configured authentication providers to log in to Cognos BI portal.

When the **Cognos** namespace under **Authentication** is clicked on, it shows a very
important option related to anonymous users' access to the Cognos connection and
web interfaces. When the Cognos BI components are installed and configured with
basic options, all users can access the Cognos connection with full permissions.
This needs to be fixed before sharing the URL with end users. Before disabling
anonymous access to Cognos BI, you must ensure that an authentication provider
has been configured and tested, and at least one user from the configured
authentication provider is a member of the built-in **Cognos** namespace system
administrators group.

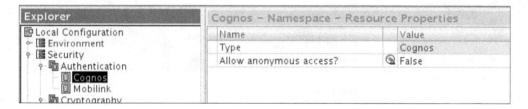

Configuring a third-party authentication provider, such as **LDAP (Lightweight Directory Access Protocol**), requires detailed configurations. For this, the Cognos manual can be referred as it gives step-by-step and detailed procedures for configuring a third-party security namespace.

Data is very important to every organization; even more important is the protection of data so that in case it is moved from one organization to another, it should be in a format that cannot be used. Once the cryptographic settings have been configured, passwords and data can be encrypted as per the scheme selected during encryption (cryptography). The following screenshot shows the general options for **Cryptography**:

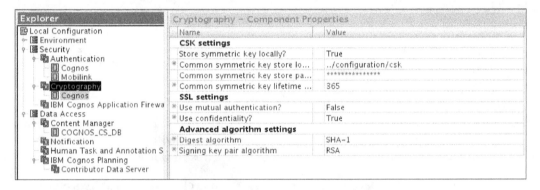

Once the **Cognos** namespace under **Cryptography** (it is a built-in namespace) is clicked on, more details are shown in the following screenshot. Note, the password must be kept in a safe place.

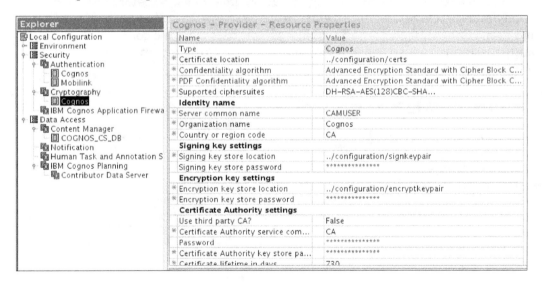

IBM Cognos Application Firewall helps the Cognos BI environment to secure any unwanted access to the system. Its task is to validate XML and web requests. The options related to the firewall are visible in the following screenshot:

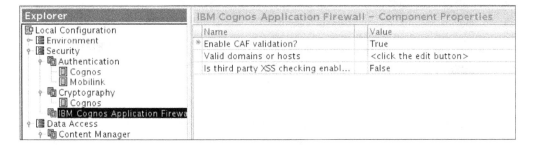

Data Access

The third section under the **Explorer** pane is **Data Access**. The services and features related to **Content Manager** (if installed on this server) appear when **Content Manager** clicked on. There is also another option to save the report outputs to a filesystem. The following screenshot shows the options:

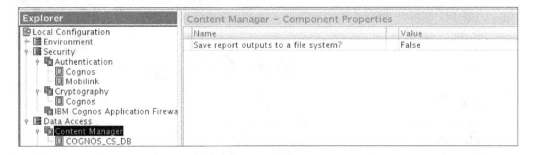

The content store database settings will appear as soon as the user clicks on the entry under **Content Manager**. These options are similar to the audit RDMBS section. The following screenshot shows the DB content store and its options:

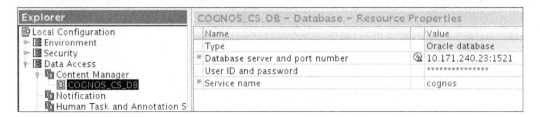

To configure the **Notification** service (e-mail), options may be noted down from the following screenshot where the SMTP outgoing e-mail is being configured:

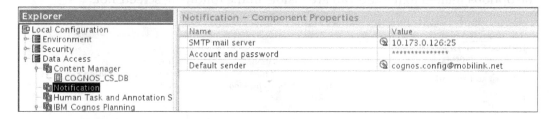

To configure the **Notification** service, you need to get the SMTP outgoing e-mail sending permissions for your Cognos server IP address from your mail server administration team. They will provide an IP address and a port number that need to be entered in the **SMTP mail server** field. The credentials must also be supplied in the next field and the default e-mails to be sent from the e-mail that is supplied in the last field.

Once all the fields are updated, the administrator can test the notification service by right-clicking on **Notification** and then clicking on the **Test** option. If all goes well, the test will be successful and an e-mail will be generated and sent to the default e-mail (default sender e-mail ID).

Explaining the Cognos Configuration window

Apart from the preceding options and features that we discussed, there are certain global options as well. To access the global options, click on **Action** from the menu and navigate to **Edit Global Configurations**. The following figure shows the window that appears when you click on the **Edit Global Configurations** option. This window has quite a few tabs to add, edit, or delete fonts, languages, currencies, locales, and some general configurations. The **Archive Location File** option sets the path to directory for saving the Cognos reports.

Summary

In this chapter, we covered the basic IBM Cognos configurations one by one. These configurations help to establish a working Cognos environment with default (and standard) options.

In the next chapter we shall go through the IBM Cognos BI Server Components.

 For detailed documentation on enhanced configurations, please refer to http://www-01.ibm.com/support/docview. wss?uid=swg27024067.

3
Managing IBM Cognos BI Server Components

When it comes to enterprise software, it must involve proper planning, design, and implementation for its success. IBM Cognos is a similar software that has been divided into multiple components, where each component has its dedicated responsibility that makes it easy to handle. In this chapter we will go through all the Cognos components and the architecture of IBM Cognos. Load balancing will also be discussed at the end of this chapter along with certain benefits of having this sort of Cognos architecture.

Cognos BI architecture

The IBM Cognos 10.2 BI architecture is separated into the following three tiers:

- Web server (gateways)
- Applications (dispatcher and Content Manager)
- Data (reporting/querying the database, content store, metric store)

Web server – gateways

The user starts a web session with Cognos to connect to the IBM Cognos Connection's web-based interface/application using the web browser (Internet Explorer and Mozilla Firefox are the currently supported browsers). This web request is sent to the web server where the Cognos gateway resides.

The gateway is a server-software program that works as an intermediate party between the web server and other servers, such as an application server. The following diagram shows the basic view of the three tiers of the Cognos BI architecture:

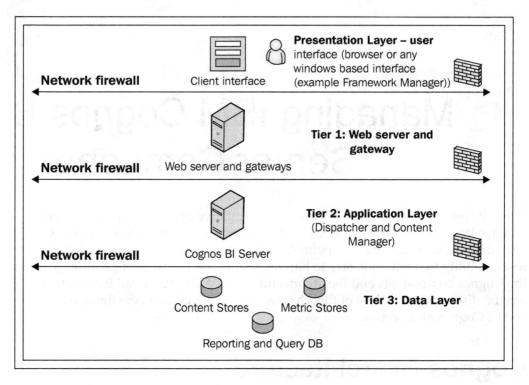

The Cognos gateway is the starting point from where a request is received and transferred to the BI Server. On receiving a request from the web server, the Cognos gateway applies encryption to the information received, adds necessary environment variables and authentication namespace, and transfers the information to the application server (or dispatcher).

Similarly, when the data has been processed and the presentation is ready, it is rendered towards the user's browser via the gateway and web server. The following diagram shows the Tier 1 layer in detail:

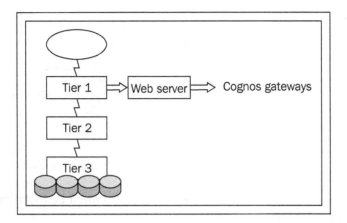

The gateways must be configured to communicate with the application component (dispatcher) in a distributed environment. To make a failover cluster, more than one BI Server may be configured.

The following types of web gateways are supported:

- CGI: This is also the default gateway. This is a basic gateway.
- ISAPI: This is for the Windows environment. It is the best for Windows **IIS (Internet Information Services)**.
- Servlet: This gateway is the best for application servers that are supporting servlets.
- Apache_mod: This gateway type may be used for the Apache server.

The following diagram shows an environment in which the web server is load balanced by two server machines:

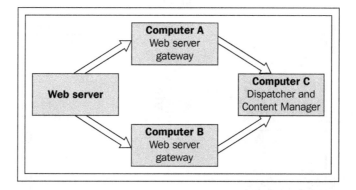

To improve performance, gateways (if more than one) must be installed and configured on separate machines.

The application tier – Cognos BI Server

The application tier comprises one or multiple BI Servers. A server's job is to run user requests, for example, queries, reports, and analysis that are received from a gateway.

The GUI environment (IBM Cognos Connection) that appears after logging in is also rendered and presented by Cognos BI Server. Another such example is the Metric Studio interface.

The BI Server must include the dispatcher and Content Manager (the Content Manager component may be separated from the dispatcher). The following diagram shows BI Server's Tier 2 in detail:

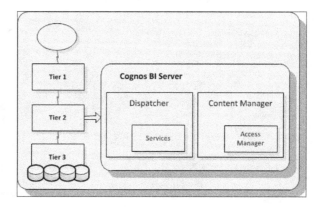

Dispatcher

The dispatcher has static handlers to many services. Each request that is received is routed to the corresponding service for further processing.

The dispatcher is also responsible for starting all the Cognos services at startup. These services include the system service, report service, report data service, presentation service, Metric Studio service, log service, job service, event management service, Content Manager service, batch report service, delivery service, and many others.

When there are multiple dispatchers in a multitier architecture, a dispatcher may also send and route requests to another dispatcher. The URIs for all dispatchers must be known to the Cognos gateway(s).

All dispatchers are registered in Content Manager (CM), making it possible for all dispatchers to know each other. A dispatcher grid is formed in this way.

To improve the system performance, multiple dispatchers must be installed but on separate computers, and the Content Manager component must also be on a separate server. The following diagram shows how multiple dispatcher servers can be added.

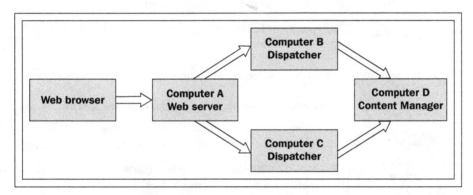

Services for the BI Server (dispatcher)

Each dispatcher has a set of services, which are listed alphabetically in the following table. When the Cognos service is started from Cognos Configuration, all services are started one by one.

The following table shows the dispatcher services and their short descriptions:

Service	Description
Agent service	Runs the agent.
Annotation service	Adds comments to reports.
Batch report service	Handles background report requests.
Content Manager cache service	Handles the cache for frequent queries to enhance performance of Content Manager.
Content Manager service	Performs DML in content store db. Cognos deployment is another task for this service.
Delivery service	Sends e-mails.
Event management service	Manages the event objects (creation, scheduling, and so on)
Graphics service	Renders graphics for other services such as the report service.
Human task service	Manages human tasks.
Index data service	For basic full-text functions for the storage and retrieval of terms and indexed summary documents.
Index search service	For search and drill-through functions, including lists of aliases and examples.
Index update service	For write, update, delete, and administration-related functions.
Job service	Runs jobs in coordination with the monitor service.
Log service	For extensive logging of the Cognos environment (file, database, remote-log server, event viewer, and system log).
Metadata service	Displays data lineage information (data source, and calculation expressions) for the Cognos studios and viewer.
Metric Studio service	This service is used for providing a user interface to the Metric Studio to monitor and manipulate system KPIs.
Migration service	Used for migration from old versions to new versions, especially series 7.
Monitor service	Works as a timer service—it manages the monitoring and running of tasks that were scheduled or marked as background tasks. Helps in failover and recovery for running tasks.

Service	Description
Presentation service	This service prepares and displays the presentation layer by converting the XML data to HTML or any other format view. IBM Cognos Connection is also prepared by this service.
Query service	Manages dynamic query requests.
Report data service	This service prepares data for other applications; for example, mobile devices, Microsoft Office, and so on.
Report service	Manages report requests. The output is displayed in IBM Cognos Connection.
System service	This service defines the BI-Bus API compliant service. It gives users more data on the BI configuration parameters.

Content Manager

Content Manager is responsible for managing report contents (customer application data, security, configurations, settings, report specifications, and report outputs). It also manages the scheduling info and other Cognos namespaces. The packages are also published with the help of Content Manager. All the information that is managed by Content Manager resides in the content-store database, which lies in the data tier.

There can be more than one Content Manager in a Cognos environment. However, the clustering of these Content Manager server deployments have to be in an active-passive mode. Only one Content Manager is active at a time, and all others are on standby. In the case of failover, the next available Content Manager becomes active. The initially, the active Content Manager will resume (when started) as the standby Content Manager. The following diagram shows how active and standby Content Managers work. The front **Content Manager** is the active Content Manager, and the boxes behind the front **Content Manager** serve as **Standby Content Manager**.

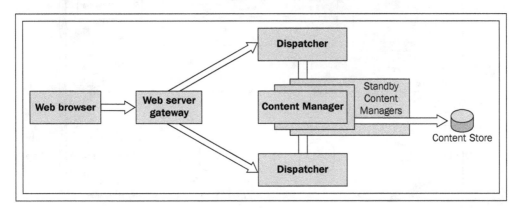

The information that Content Manager stores and manipulates includes:

- Data related to the server configuration, for example, directory information, namespaces, contacts, DLs, data sources, and other namespaces such as printers
- Information related to reports (report properties, permissions, outputs, and report specifications)
- Packages (information related to reports, dimensional packages, and metric packages)
- Agents (schedules, events, conditions, and e-mail delivery info)
- User information (personal information, and the **My Folder** and **My Pages** areas)
- Workspace information
- Language-related information (for multilingual capabilities)

Content Manager also performs general functions (cut, copy, paste, delete, update, query, refresh, add, and content import/export). Content Manager has an internal process called **Access Manager**, which is the security manager of Cognos. The typical features of Access Manager include encryption, authentication, and authorization.

Cognos uses the default certificate authority that may be overridden by any other third-party certificate authority. The following diagram shows the detailed scenario for a load balancer:

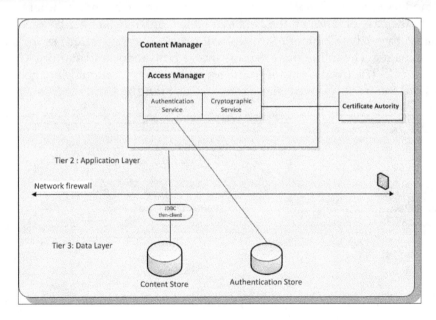

Data tier – the content store, query/reporting database, and metric store

The third-tier (data tier) contains the following:

- Content store (single instance)
- Metric store (multiple instances)
- Data sources (for variety of RDBMS)

The content store

The content store database contains data that Cognos needs to function properly. This includes all the information discussed earlier in the *Content Manager* section, including report specifications, published packages, connection information for data sources, information about the external namespace, the Cognos namespace itself, and information about scheduling and bursting reports. For Cognos Mobile, the service may access the content store using a separate database client, if it is not using the Content Manager path.

The content store is the database for Content Manager. The content store database is configured via the Cognos Configuration window, and all the tables in the schema are initially almost blank.

Data sources that can be accessed through IBM Cognos BI include databases, dimensional or OLAP cubes, flat files, and other physical data stores. They also include connection information necessary for accessing the data. Basically these are the connection namespaces that contain all the information required to connect to the reporting databases.

If the content store was also selected during installation of the Cognos components, a DB2 content store is created and configured with default options. The Content store is an optional component during installation; if it is not selected, the administrator has to configure a content store explicitly after the installation of the Cognos components using the IBM Cognos BI configuration window. If the content store was selected during installation and the administrator wants to shift the content store to some other RDBMS, the current content store has to be removed first before adding a new content store.

The metric store

A metric store database contains the content for metric packages. A metric store also contains Metric Studio settings, such as user preferences. Cognos BI uses RDBMS for its metric store, and can be configured to use the same database that the content store is using. The following diagram shows the typical architecture of the content and metric stores in the Cognos environments:

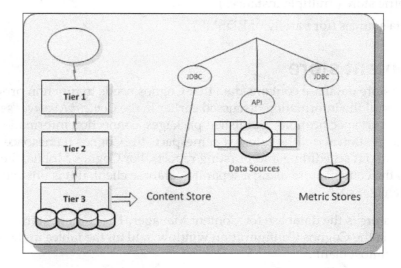

Data sources

Data sources are used as namespaces that contain the connection strings, settings, and parameters required to connect to a data model, such as RDBMS, plain but flat and organized data files (such as CSV files), cubes, and other data models.

Data sources can be viewed or modified under **IBM Cognos Administration** under the **Configurations** section. The Framework Manager also has the capability to create data source connections on the Cognos BI environment that the framework manager configurations are pointing to.

Cognos BI 10.2, like its earlier versions, supports a vast range of connectivity with almost all relational databases. Cognos BI Server uses these data sources to connect to databases in order to query data. Most of the data sources require either clients or connectors to be installed on the Cognos BI application server.

Connectivity using JDBC connectors is also possible. Dynamic Query Mode is a new feature in Cognos 10.1 and is now the recommended method of connectivity.

Cognos BI may also be used with **Enterprise Information Integration** (**EII**) products, for example, Virtual View Manager, which provides reachability to some additional data sources such as JDBC, Open XML, WSDL, and LDAP. It is well optimized and gives a better performance.

Cognos BI interfaces

Cognos BI provides many interfaces. A list of these interfaces along with their brief descriptions is mentioned in the following sections.

Zero footprint – IBM Cognos web-based interfaces for users

The following sections discuss the web-based interfaces available to Cognos users. The following sections discuss the web-based interfaces available to Cognos users. For a user to gain access to these interfaces, proper capabilities must be assigned to the user, There are two ways, either explicitly add the user to allowed users for every interface (for example, query studio, reports studio, cognos connection etc.) or add the user to built-in roles or groups in Cognos security namespace. Web-based interfaces include the following interfaces.

IBM Cognos Connection

IBM Cognos Connection is a portal with many features available to a user depending on the permission that is assigned. From Cognos Connection, the user may access any other interface (any studio, administration section), provided that the permissions allow the user to access it.

Users may access the preferences, other portals, public, or my folders. Users may also run any available Cognos content.

IBM Cognos Administration

Only administrators and power users may access this section. Full permissions are available to users that belong to the **System Administrator** group in the Cognos security namespace. From the Cognos Administration portal, users have easy access to the management functions, Cognos environment, and system parameters.

Cognos Query Studio

This studio is used for ad hoc reporting. Users with a basic knowledge of Cognos and reporting can easily use this studio to prepare a report. The functionality of this studio is limited compared to the Report Studio.

Cognos Report Studio

In order to develop and create professional reports, this studio is available with a bundle of options. Authors have access to this studio.

Cognos Analysis Studio

The Analysis Studio is used for detailed analysis and dimensioning extensive OLAP. It is fast and needs dimension tables to be created first.

Cognos Event Studio

The Event Studio is used to create agents that monitor a particular event to trigger before some work is done.

Cognos Metric Studio

Custom score cards may be created in Metric Studio. This is used for monitoring and analyzing.

Cognos Workspace

Cognos Workspace is used to create interactive workspaces using the available Cognos reports and other contents.

Cognos Workspace Advanced

Advanced data can be explored and used in reports.

Windows-based interfaces for users

Unlike web-based interfaces, there are certain interfaces (such as the ones listed in the following sections) that need separate installation and configuration.

Cognos Framework Manager

Cognos Framework Manager is used for modeling the data that will be available in Cognos Package.

Cognos Metric Designer

Cognos Metric Designer is also a modeling tool that is used to create extracts. Later, it is used in Metric Studio.

Cognos Map Manager

For creating map-supported reports, Cognos Map Manager needs to import map-related data and labels.

Cognos BI for Microsoft Office

With the configuration of Cognos BI for Microsoft Office, users are able to access Cognos data from within all of the Microsoft Office programs.

Cognos Transformer

Cognos Transformer is used to create PowerCubes.

Cognos Insight

Cognos Insight is used to analyze data, which helps in decision making. Creating workspaces in the Cognos Insight tool also helps in decision making.

Things to remember

While installing Cognos BI and performing the initial configurations, few things that must be kept in mind are mentioned as follows:

- In distributed environments, Content Manager(s) must know the location of its content stores.
- In distributed environments, the application tier components (dispatcher) must know the location of Content Manager(s).
- Gateway computer(s) must know the location of at least one dispatcher.
- Cryptographic properties (passwords) must be the same on all computers, otherwise communication failure will occur. For this purpose, the gateway server must be configured at the end.

- After completing the configurations, the services on the Content Manager computer must start first.

- Do not use the same content store for multiple Content Managers running in the active mode; for example, two totally separate BI Servers that are running with all the components installed on the same machine and configured with the same content store. In this case, chances are that the content store will get corrupted. If the Cognos BI applications are running in a distributed environment, all Content Managers must use the same content store; but only one Content Manager is active at a time, and the remaining will work as standby Content Managers.

- When all the components have been installed and configured on the server(s), it is important to start Content Manager first (the one you want to make active). The remaining (if any) Content Managers must be started after that.

- The other components may be configured and started after the Content Manager.

- The server specified in the external dispatcher field URI on the gateway server should be the last server component that is started.

- For a Windows environment, install and configure all the server components before you install the Windows components.

- When services on Cognos servers are stopped, it is important to follow a sequence. The application tier components must be stopped first, then standby Content Manager(s) (if any), and then the active Content Manager.

- The easiest way to start Cognos is from the Windows command shell. Enter the NET START "IBM Cognos" command. To stop Cognos, use NET STOP "IBM Cognos". This will start or stop the services in correct order.

Load balancing

Multiple instances of the IBM Cognos BI components must be used to balance the loading of requests.

At the level of dispatcher, load balancing is automatic in a distributed environment, as shown in the following diagram:

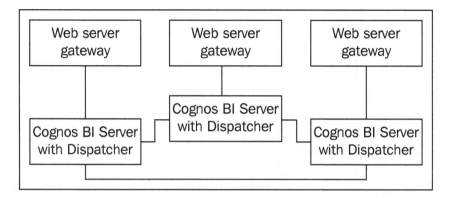

Load balancing can be implemented without an external load-balancing mechanism. Check out the load balancing options in the following diagram:

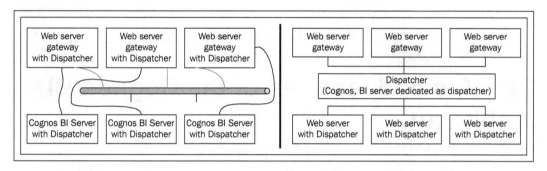

The load may be balanced with an external load-balancing mechanism. For an example, see the following diagram:

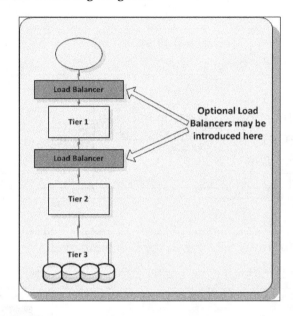

Benefits and features of the Cognos BI architecture

The benefits and features of the Cognos BI architecture are as follows:

- It provides zero footprint on a client machine (in other words, it takes no space on a client's machine)
- It supports load balancing not only by scaling up, but also by scaling out by adding new server-machine instances, even without an external load balancer
- It integrates with web farms
- It is platform independent
- It has a common dispatcher
- It is open and extensible
- It supports the leading RDBMS to persist data that is related to content management and reporting
- It is multilingual

The information provided in this chapter was gathered and verified with the official manual of IBM Cognos BI.

Summary

This chapter covered the IBM Cognos BI architecture. By now you must be familiar with the single tier and multitier architectures and a variety of features and options that Cognos provides.

The next chapter will cover Cognos Administration Portal in detail, including all the features and functionalities covered by IBM Cognos BI 10.2.

4
Administration Portal

A Cognos BI administrator has to spend most of his/her time on the web interface looking after the different KPIs and the performance of Cognos BI along with making certain changes that are required to be performed in a routine manner. We shall be discussing the Cognos BI Administration portal in detail in this chapter. The following major topics will be covered in this chapter:

- The Status tab
- The Security tab
- The Configuration tab
- The Index Search tab

For detailed information and understanding of these subjects, a Cognos BI 10.2 manual may be referred.

Power of the Cognos BI Administration portal

IBM Cognos 10.2 BI gives a vast range of options to Cognos BI administrators. Talking about subjects ranging from the initial configuration to routine configuration and the security of the current system status, Cognos BI covers each section of administration. Understanding the Cognos BI administration is a piece of cake, but when it comes to the production environment, performing administrative tasks is a big responsibility. For this purpose, Cognos BI has many features, such as security, logging, and auditing.

With IBM Cognos BI Administration, system administrators are able to manage their business analytics systems proactively. This way, they also prevent problems before they arise. The administrator is able to know the BI system usage scheme, environment, and business expectations. He/she is able to resolve and prevent issues by knowing the system KPIs. This is done by making thresholds by way of tracking and evolving over time. For example, a system-level metric provides the number of current user sessions logged on to the system. Another metric provides the number of requests received at a specific point in time. It can express the peak times (busy hours) of the system where spikes are expected. It also helps in scheduling the batch jobs at appropriate times.

The number of queue requests is another metric that provides the number of requests that have gone through the queue. The higher the number of requests in the queue, the higher is the volume of system activity at an instance.

Another metric, called longest time in queue, explains the longest time that a request has been in the queue. The longer a request stays in the queue, the higher the system activity.

With frequent observation of these usage patterns, a Cognos BI system administrator can know if this is a regular activity or an issue that needs to be addressed.

To have a better idea of the system health, there are many other system metrics that explain the current condition of a system. If these metrics appear to be problematic, then fine-tuning certain counters helps, depending upon which KPI is affected. The administrator may also need to add more server nodes to the current Cognos farm in case there is a capacity issue and the current servers are not capable enough to handle the load. Three of these metrics are: the successful requests per minute, the number of processed requests per dispatcher, and the percentage of failed requests. With all these system metrics, their thresholds, and high and low watermarks defined, one can have a true picture of the system status. The following screenshot shows the welcome page of IBM Cognos BI 10.2 when a user with administration privileges logs in. If the user is in the IBM Cognos Connection area, the responsibility can also be switched by using the **Launch** link from the top-right corner of the web page.

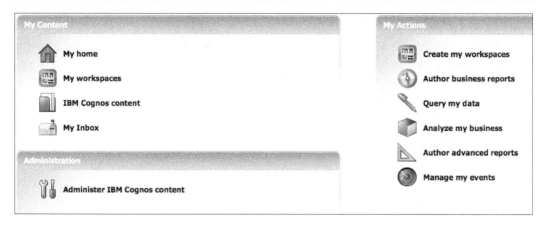

We will now discuss each Administration environment section in detail.

The following screenshot shows the four tabs of the IBM Cognos Administration environment:

The Status tab

One of the main responsibilities of an administrator is to keep an eye on what is going on in the system currently. For this, the **Status** tab of the Cognos BI Administration portal is of great help. It gives a nearly true picture of what really is happening in the Cognos environment at the moment. Let's now discuss each and every portion of this tab in detail. Once the administrator has logged in and navigated to the administration section, the default page that is shown is the **Status** tab. The screenshot present under the *Current Activities* heading shows how it looks.

Current Activities

The default view of the **Status** tab (as shown in the following screenshot) is **Current Activities**, which shows the currently running background activities. **Background activities** are the batch processes.

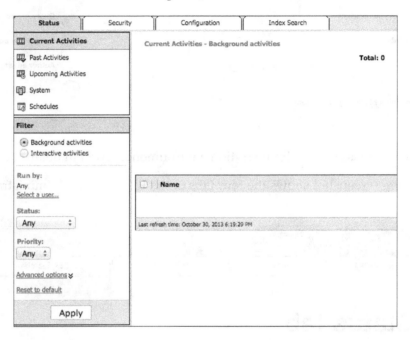

All the currently running background activities are shown on the right-hand side of the portal page. The following screenshot shows a view of the running background (batch) activities. The administrator may cancel or suspend these activities from the appropriate options available in the drop-down arrow next to the job name or on the top-right corner of the **Current Activities** pane.

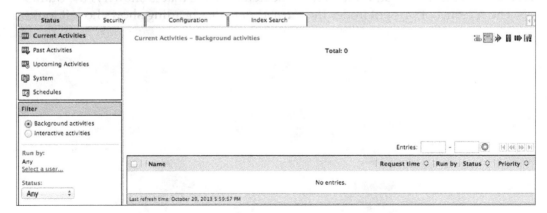

Past Activities

Similarly, the past activities may also be viewed from the **Past Activities** area
of the **Status** tab. This gives a picture of how many activities were completed
and how many failed. For the failed activities, the details of the reasons for
failure may be viewed.

Upcoming Activities

To know more about the upcoming tasks, the Cognos BI Administration portal
contains an area that focuses on future activities. This option also gives users an idea
of the peak time of the system in terms of scheduled activities. Using this section,
the administrator may shift the reports and activities to an appropriate time when
system utilization is low. The following screenshot shows **Upcoming Activities** and
its detailed view:

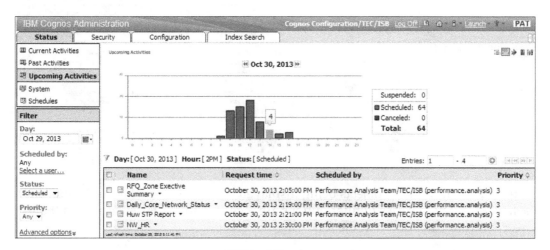

By hovering over the bars of the chart area, the count of activities running in that
particular time period can also be seen although the y axis of the chart also provides
the approximate information.

Schedules

All reports, jobs, events, queries, and tasks in general that are required to be run at specific times appear in this section. Every item that can be scheduled has a separate icon for scheduling in IBM Cognos Connection. The user also requires permissions to schedule items. All items that will run in the future can be seen in **Upcoming Activities**. The items currently running appear in the **Current Activities** section and of course, the items that have already run will appear in the **Past Activities** section. An item that is currently running, or those that may be consuming too many system resources, can be cancelled or set to low priority from the **Schedules** section. The following screenshot shows the **Schedules** window:

To reduce the number of objects being displayed or to quickly isolate and focus on particular objects, a series of filter options are included in the **Filter** section in the lower-left frame as shown in the following screenshot:

System

One of the most important areas of the **Status** tab is **System**. This area shows the KPIs of the system, which that are called metrics. A simplified one-tier architecture, where every Cognos BI component runs on one machine, will have one server appearing in this area. Once all the appropriate metrics are defined, we will be able get the actual historical condition of **System**. The following screenshot shows the **System** area:

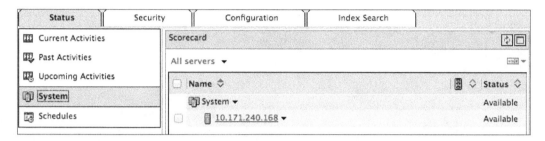

This area is used for getting an overall picture of how the Cognos BI system is performing. It is done by status indicators on a dashboard. We can divide the system task area into three sub-sections:

- **Scorecard**: This is the middle area that displays a summarized view of the overall components' health currently in the environment.

- **Metrics**: This list of all metrics along with their ratings and scores is present at the top-right area just below the Cognos BI Administration portal header. By default, the overall environment metrics are shown, but one can filter these out on the basis of custom criteria.

- **Settings**: This is the settings section that appears on the bottom-right area of the portal. The values shown in this area are for information purposes only. It gives the configuration details of the object selected.

The next screenshot shows what we have just discussed.

By default, all metrics are not set; we have to set each metric on the basis of the requirements that we have. There is a long list of requirements for all metrics. The summarized view shows values on the basis of configured metrics. Therefore, these metrics have to be configured manually and carefully.

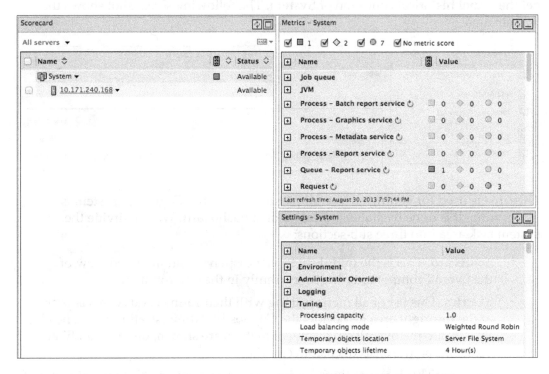

In the previous screenshot, as you can see, the system health appearing in the **Scorecard** area is shown as problematic. However, there is only one metric that is currently in red. If there is any metric that is a problem, the main scorecard view will be shown as problematic in order to pull the attention of the administrator to the area where there is something wrong, that is, it's time to troubleshoot.

To summarize the **System** area, we have come to know that this is used to get an understanding of the current situation of the system, the happenings, the problems, the tasks that have been completed, and a look at the ones to follow.

The Security tab

The next tab is the **Security** tab. It also has different sections, which will be discussed briefly. In enterprise applications, security requires consideration as almost all organizations require data to be hidden from other organizations, especially reports such as the ones Cognos BI produces. Even in the same organization, different divisions, and departments within the divisions, also tend to hide data from others. Another consideration includes the people who were involved in a particular task in an enterprise system. In order to track down all these features, Cognos BI has also added the security module. To manage different security needs, the namespaces following the different sections within the **Security** tab are used. The following screenshot shows the view when the **Security** tab is selected:

Users, groups, and roles

This area gives us the freedom to manage groups, roles, and users. There is a built-in Cognos namespace that contains predefined roles and groups for convenience. The following screenshot shows the built-in roles and groups. The name of each group or role will define its purpose. These groups have been created in a way that the required permissions and capabilities have already been added to these groups. This means that if we want to give a user access to Report Studio, we need to add him/her to the built-in **Authors** group, at least in order for the user to view and use Report Studio.

The custom folders, groups, and roles can also be created and used.

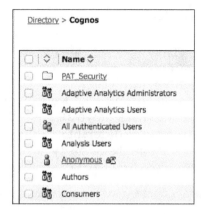

In addition to this, users must be added to these roles and groups from some external, third-party security namespace, for example, LDAP, Active directory, or Custom Java Security Namespace. When users log in, they get a separate private profile and a private document-keeping area called `My Folders`.

Capabilities

This is a collection of Cognos portal features that can be assigned to roles, groups, or users. The users added to a particular group or role having some feature permissions can also be controlled globally from the **Capabilities** area. The following screenshot shows the list of capabilities. The capabilities shown as underlined or with links may contain nested options.

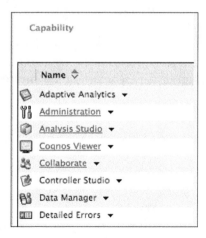

If we click on the **Scheduling** capability, it will lead us to all the available nested options or those that may be assigned to some user, group, or role as shown in the following screenshot:

User interface profiles

IBM Cognos BI provides separate custom user interfaces that contain separate features for report authoring. The two modes that are supported are as follows:

- **Professional Mode**: This is available in Report Studio and gives users access to all features and functionalities. The feature-rich reports that can be developed in this mode include charts, maps, lists, and more.

- **Express Mode**: This is available in the advanced Cognos BI workspace, and it provides an interface for business users who can create crosstabs, lists, and charts.

To support the preceding modes, the Administration portal provides two profiles listed under the **Security** tab. The following screenshot shows **User Interface Profiles**:

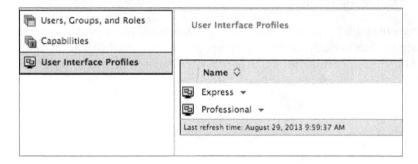

The Configuration tab

The third tab shown on the IBM Cognos BI Administration portal is the **Configuration** tab. The author role also has this tab available along with the **Status** tab, but no other tab (for example, the **Security** tab, a detailed **Configuration** tab, or the **Index Search** tab) is available to authors. The administrators have this tab fully populated with options. We shall be discussing each option one by one. The following screenshot shows the default view when the **Configuration** tab is selected:

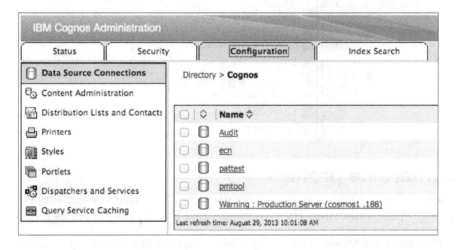

Data Source Connections

This is the first option that appears by default when the **Configuration** tab is clicked. Here the administrators may define data source connections for reporting databases. These data sources are then used by the Cognos content. There are a variety of database connection options that include all the major RDBMS databases, for example, DB2, Informix, SQL Server, and Oracle. The server hosting the Cognos application may also require additional clients or connectors to connect to the respective database systems.

Data sources may be defined using the Cognos wizard after providing the appropriate parameters. As shown in the previous screenshot, there are many Cognos Data source connections defined, each of which points to either different databases or different schemas within a database.

Content management

Everything appearing in a Cognos connection and administration portal can be named content. In order to manage this content in terms of backups, content maintenance, and index updates, the Cognos Administration portal provides a separate section where these options are available. The following screenshot shows the default view:

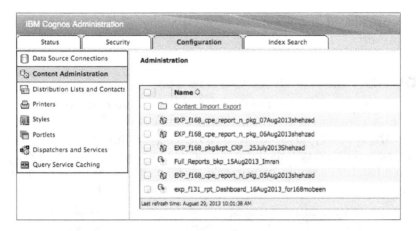

All content (for example, packages, reports, jobs, schedules, security items, queries, report views, and contacts) can be backed up using the deployment feature. We can export all the content to a compressed archive and then shift it to other media or another server where we can import the content. The following screenshot shows the archives that are placed in the deployment folder and are available to be imported:

The following screenshot shows all the available options for content management. It includes the export, import, index, and maintenance tasks for content management.

The archives are placed at `<Cognos install path>/deployments` for both export and import.

Distribution Lists and Contacts

Distribution lists (DLs) are used to send a report to more than one recipient at at a time. DLs may contain users, groups, roles, contacts, or other DLs. If a recipient is not part of the IBM Cognos security system, a contact for that person can be created. The report delivery fails if there is no read access on an e-mail recipient chosen from a list, for example, group, role, or DL. The following screenshot shows a few contacts created under the **Distribution Lists and Contacts** section:

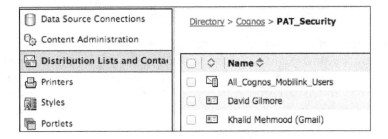

Printers

Cognos also supports the addition and configuration of **Printers**. This option is used in **Schedules** as shown in the following screenshot:

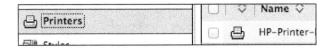

Styles

It is like using a portal skin (or CSS styles) when it comes to Cognos styles. By default, there are a few styles available, but depending upon the requirements of a company, these styles are customizable. Companies can add their color schemes, fonts, logos, and images to specific portions of the portal as shown in the following screenshot:

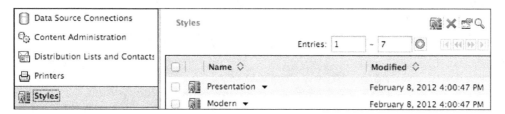

Portlets

We can define a portlet as a way to display web content as part of another portal page. Cognos includes built-in portlets along with some other portlets. Cognos portlets include **Navigator**, **Viewer**, **Search**, **Content**, **Extended Applications**, **Utility**, and **Dashboard**. The following screenshot shows the configuration section for portlets inside the **Portlets** tab:

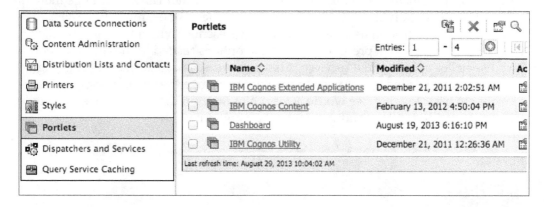

Query Service Caching

Cognos BI has the feature of using previously run results of queries and reports. This helps in the enhancement of the system performance by avoiding queries reaching reach the database layer. This is an intelligent feature that also takes care of user security. The following screenshot shows the **Query Service Caching** tab. The Cognos administrator has the privilege to either clear or write this cache.

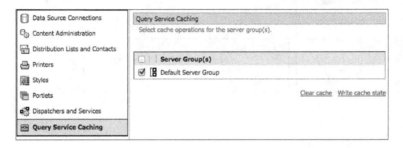

Dispatchers and Services

One of the most important sections of the **Configuration** tab is that an administrator can configure different options of all the dispatchers running in the environment with the help of options included in this section. The administrator can also change the configuration of an individual service for any dispatcher. For example, if we click on any dispatcher and click on its properties, we are presented with a few tabs. By clicking on the **Settings** tab, we are presented with more options related to the configuration of the dispatcher or individual services. All the services are categorized as **Logging**, **Environment**, or **Tuning**. If, for instance, we opt to change the level for logging from no logging to basic logging, we would select **Logging** from the dropdown and change the desired logging levels as shown in the following screenshot:

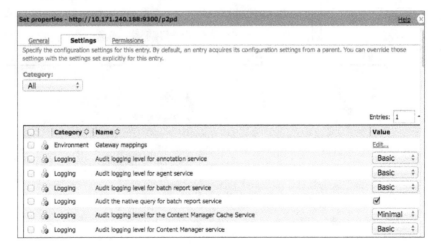

The Index Search tab

Cognos uses index search as the default search capability. It is mandatory to configure the index search before using it. At least one index should be available to Cognos. There are a lot of options to configure the index search. Please see the following screenshot of the **Index Search** tab:

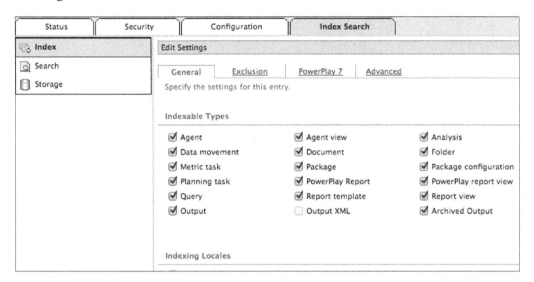

Summary

This chapter covered the IBM Cognos BI Administration portal briefly. Of course, each section in this chapter requires detailed discussion in order for us to fully understand it, but we hope the previous discussion, though brief, gave an idea about the different features of the Cognos Administration portal.

In the next chapter, we shall discuss ways to secure the IBM Cognos environment and the features available to secure the IBM Cognos BI environment.

5
Securing IBM Cognos BI

Every professional application must have stable and easy-to-implement security features. An environment must be reliable wherein every user is free of worries about security. IBM Cognos BI provides an environment that is trustable. By the end of this chapter, you should be able to secure the IBM Cognos BI environment, recognize security policies, define authentication and authorization in Cognos, and identify the Cognos BI security model. To do this, we will discuss the following topics in detail:

- Security architecture
- Managing authentication providers
- Overcoming the initial security
- Permissions management
- Secured features, functionalities, and capabilities
- Cognos firewall and logging
- Single Sign-on (SSO)

The following screenshot shows the area we will be focusing on in this chapter. The **Security** tab is highlighted.

The IBM Cognos BI Security architecture

The IBM Cognos BI Security architecture involves authentication, authorization, encryption, certificates, and of course, administration. Every area focuses on its unique subject, for example, encryption deals with encrypting the data that flows between different machines. Both encryption and decryption algorithms are selected and implemented when Cognos is started on the Content Manager machine. The following diagram shows the architecture of security in IBM Cognos BI:

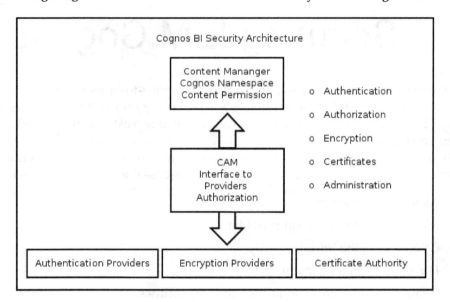

Managing authentication providers

To manage users in IBM Cognos BI, it must be linked with a third-party authentication provider. An authentication provider defines users, groups, and privileges/roles. Authentication providers store the basic information of a user, for example, username, password, e-mail ID, preferences, and group settings. Once an authentication provider is linked with the IBM Cognos BI environment, the entries of authentication providers and their basic information can be used by IBM Cognos BI for authentication, e-mail ID, and so on. Furthermore, the entries (users, groups, and roles) are not copied to the Cognos BI environment; rather, they are referred.

Cognos BI supports a vast range of third-party authentication providers, which may be configured using the IBM Cognos BI Configuration window. Every authentication provider has its own set of rules for mapping the different fields of Cognos BI with those of authentication providers. The following authentication providers are supported:

- LDAP
- Custom Java provider
- IBM Cognos Series 7
- eTrust SiteMinder
- SAP
- RACF
- Microsoft Active Directory

The following screenshot shows the security settings where an authentication provider (using LDAP) has been added in the IBM Cognos Configuration window:

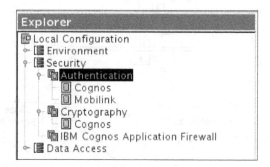

One or multiple authentication providers can be used by performing the respective configurations in the IBM Cognos BI Configuration window. A list of authentication providers is available on the IBM Cognos BI login page if multiple providers have been configured. If no authentication provider is configured, the Cognos BI environment is used anonymously. An inactive namespace can be made active by reconfiguring it in the IBM Cognos BI Configuration window with the original (old) settings.

An authentication provider if deleted from the IBM Cognos BI Configuration window becomes inactive in the Administration portal under the **Security** tab. Users with the System Administrator role can even delete it from the content store. The following diagram shows a built-in Cognos namespace and a third-party LDAP authentication provider namespace:

It must be noted here that all the contents of the **My Folders** area will be lost for all users who belong to this authentication provider. The authentication process is shown in the following diagram:

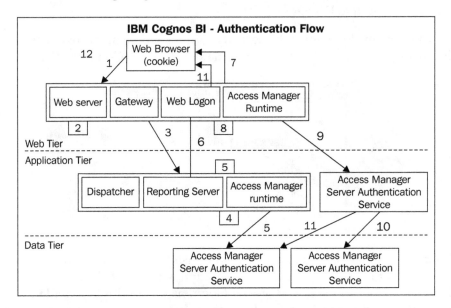

Cognos BI authorization

The IBM Cognos BI authorization process gives permissions to users, allowing them to perform the actions assigned to them. Authorization is a mechanism of giving or revoking access to information.

The permissions are assigned based on Cognos content. Data in the content store is stored in the form of a hierarchy. Therefore, the read, write, execute, traverse, and set policy permissions are available. Each of these permissions may either be allowed or denied. The **deny** action overrides the **allow** action wherever specified. Due to the hierarchy factor, the permissions may be granted to the object and all its child objects. Every new content will get the default permissions from its parent. If overriding is required, the **Override** option in the **Permissions** tab of **Content Properties** may be used.

Cognos namespace

When Cognos BI services are started for the first time, content store initialization takes place and many default features are created. IBM Cognos BI provides a built-in, ready-to-use namespace for managing almost all functions of security in particular. The namespace also contains functions of other areas, for example, data sources, contacts, and DLs. This namespace cannot be removed; however, it may be renamed. The implementation of security policies is made very easy by using this namespace. It also supports the creation of folders, new groups, and roles. For example, if different groups of organizations require different permissions and capabilities, all that needs to be done is to create groups in the Cognos namespace and add the DLs or groups from the authentication provider to this newly created group.

The Cognos namespace also contains a default user profile that contains all preferences and settings that will apply to all new users when they log in for the first time as shown in the following screenshot:

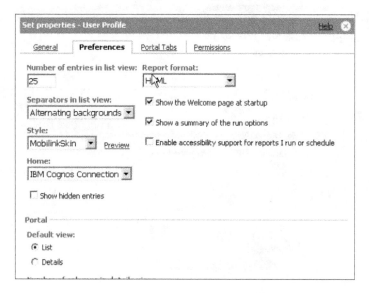

If a company requires using a set of preferences and a default company skin (CSS or style) for its Cognos BI users, this feature may be used. If any user is logged in to Cognos BI before the implementation of this setting, the profile will not acquire the new settings. This is done by launching the Administration Portal, navigating to the **Security** tab, and clicking on **Cognos Namespace** under **Users, Groups and Roles**. Click on the **Edit default profile** option in the toolbar to set the default user's profile.

Users can also change the default settings that are set by the company administrators later on if required, and the permission is then allowed.

Overcoming the initial security

Once Cognos BI has been installed and configured with the basic options and one or multiple authentication providers, it is vulnerable to the end users because every user is by default an administrator of the IBM Cognos BI environment. This is because the built-in role **Everyone** is added to the members list of the built-in **System Administrators** role/group. It must be removed from the unwanted built-in roles available in the Cognos namespace of the **Security** tab in the IBM Cognos BI Administration portal. Trusted users (from any authentication provider) must be added to the **System Administrators** role before removing **Everyone** from the **System Administrators** role. As in the following screenshot, custom members have been added. One role has been added from the Cognos namespace and two users added from the third-party authentication provider:

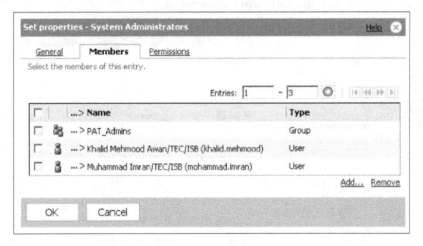

A few configurations also need to be done in the IBM Cognos BI Configuration window as shown in the following screenshot. Unwanted users from authentication providers may be blocked by setting the **Restrict access to members of built-in namespace** property to **true**.

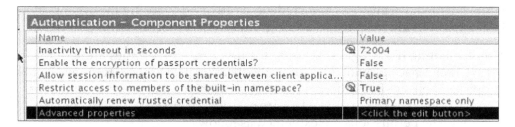

If the setting shown in the following diagram is kept to **True**, users can log in to Cognos without providing any credentials.

You must make sure that proper permissions have been given to all users, especially when authentication providers are added to Cognos BI. The **Everyone** role is also a member of a few other built-in roles; it may be removed if required.

IBM Cognos Application Firewall

IBM Cognos Application Firewall (CAF) is configured in the Cognos Configuration window to supplement security. If it is enabled, all requests (HTTP and XML) are analyzed, modified, and validated before being processed by gateways or dispatchers. Buffer overflows and cross-site scripting attacks are the most common forms of malicious data. IBM Cognos Application Firewall is enabled by default, and it is recommended against disabling it. The following screenshot shows the configurations of Firewall, where we can enable or disable the firewall:

IBM Cognos Application Firewall - Component Properties	
Name	Value
* Enable CAF validation?	True
Valid domains or hosts	<click the edit button>
Is third party XSS checking enabl...	False

Permission management

Every organization, of course, has multiple divisions and departments with a focus on one area. In an environment where Cognos BI has been implemented and all teams do not want other teams to access their data, Cognos BI security permissions are implemented. Permissions and credentials are used to secure the organization's data. Permissions are assigned to users, groups, or roles for content.

For implementing IBM Cognos Security, the users, groups, or roles are selected from either the namespace provided by the authentication provider or from the Cognos namespace. There are five different types of permissions that may be granted or revoked. If both `granted` and `revoked` are selected, then `revoke/deny` will be overridden. The permissions are explained as follows:

- **Read**: With this permission granted, properties for content may be viewed
- **Write**: With this permission granted, users can modify the properties of an entry, create entries in a container, delete an entry, and modify report specifications
- **Execute**: Users with this permission granted can process/run the entry
- **Set Policy**: Users with this permission granted may read and change the security options of an entry
- **Traverse**: Users with this permission granted can access the contents of a folder but cannot change or run anything

Users must have the **Traverse** option set in order to see the entries in a folder. Inheritance to child entries in the Cognos connection is also supported, and is a core feature for security implementation. Assign a read, write, and execute permission for a Cognos group or role, and assign that group or role the required permission to run, execute, or modify the content. The following screenshot shows items included in the built-in Cognos namespace:

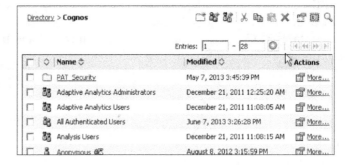

In the preceding screenshot, you can see the built-in Cognos roles along with a self-created folder.

Content security management – an example

As an example, let's consider that there is a requirement from an organization department A that they want to create a folder (CognosRpts) in the Cognos BI Connection window, which is accessible to all organizations but with the limitation that only their department should be able to modify the contents of that folder. Department B should be able to only access and run the reports to view the results of reports. Department C should only be able to access what is available in that folder, and not be able to modify or run the report.

In this scenario, we will first create a few groups or roles in the Cognos namespace under the **Security** tab. Let's create a folder and name it Test_Folder. We will create the new test folder, role, and group within Test_Folder. Now let's create three groups named **Department A**, **Department B**, and **Department C**. We will add the required users (or groups or roles) to these groups as and when required. Since our requirement was to allow Department A's users to be administrator users (with read, write, and execute permissions), first we will add all the required users to the **Department A** group. This may be done by opening **Set Properties** of the **Department A** group, opening the **Members** tab, and then adding users from any of the authentication providers (added using LDAP, AD, and so on). Even whole groups can be added to this self-created group.

Once we have added our required users to all these three groups: **Department A, Department B,** and **Department C**, we can proceed to the next step. This step is very important as here we will assign the permissions. We will now navigate to the CognosRpts folder and set its properties. In its **Permissions** tab, we will add all the three departments and assign the desired privileges. In **Security Rights** next to the **Department A** line, we will allow all permissions by selecting all the **Allow** checkboxes. In the **Department B** line, we will only check the **Traverse, Read,** and **Execute** checkboxes in order to meet the requirements. In the line next to **Department C**, we will only allow the **Traverse** permission. Next, the **Apply** button needs to be clicked. Now, the users of **Department A** have full rights to the CognosRpts folder; the users of **Department B** can read, traverse, and execute the contents of the CognosRpts folder; and the users of **Departments C** can only see the contents of CognosRpts.

Secured features, functionalities, and capabilities

To segregate functions for different types of users, Cognos BI has a secured function. Cognos BI already has predefined roles and groups defined under the **Security** tab within the Cognos namespace. At the backend, these capabilities have been assigned to different built-in security functions and features. If some change is required in any capability, it may be configured in the **Capability** area under the **Security** tab.

Capabilities are defined along with the built-in groups and roles when Content Manager is initialized for the first time. The permissions tell you which predefined roles or groups have access to which secure function and feature.

To see which capabilities a user has, a list of secure functions is available when you navigate to **My Preferences | Personal (Capabilities)**. A few capabilities are shown in the following screenshot:

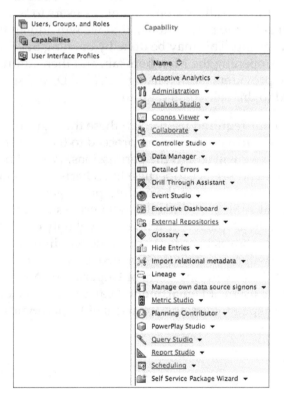

Single Sign-on

While using multiple Cognos applications, it may be irritating to provide credentials to each application. Rather, providing credentials to one application and also using them in other trusted applications can also save time. For this, the famous **Single Sign-on** (**SSO**) is used. When SSO is active, the prompt for authentication does not appear, but users are logged in automatically. SSO for the IBM Cognos components can be achieved by configuring the **External Identity** mapping property. For more information on this, the IBM Cognos official manual, *Installation and Configuration*, may be referred to as SSO has many options for configuration.

Summary

This chapter covered IBM Cognos BI Security briefly. By now, users should have a good understanding of the security features that Cognos BI provides.

In the next chapter we will be discussing the IBM Cognos BI drill-through definitions.

6
Drill-through Definitions

Almost every organization has a hierarchical structure, and every level is concerned about its level of data and reports in that hierarchy. For example, a CEO or a company president will be looking at the overall picture of revenues, sales, and expenses. The next level will be concerned about the divisional-level reports and so on. Drill through is very handy in such cases. We shall discuss the following topics related to drill through in this chapter:

- Overview of the drill-through feature
- How to create a drill-through feature/definition

Overview of the drill-through feature

Drill through defines a group of linked reports that may be navigated in a single session (preferably) in such a way that the session, context, and user focus is not affected while performing data analysis and exploring information. The drill-through feature also assists in creating BI (business intelligence) advanced reports and applications that may constitute or span across multiple views and reports.

An example here will help you understand the drill-through definitions in a better way. Consider that we have a dashboard that shows a summary of region-wise customer churn. Now consider that there are five regions, of which only one region is highly affecting the customer-churn KPI. In a drill-through application or report, a user will be provided with a link. Once the user clicks on the link, a new report will come up with the results of the churn trend of that region. Drill through may be applied on multiple fields of a report, resulting in viewing of the data from different aspects.

In a drill-through phenomenon, one report sends information to other reports as parameters. In other words, the drill-through access works by passing information from the source object (usually a report) to the target object (another report). You specify what will be passed from the source report by having the system match the information from the selection context of the source report to the content of the target report (dynamic drill through) or by defining parameters in the target (parameterized drill through). In other words, a package drill through lets you navigate to a target report from any source report that uses the same package. A package can have multiple drill-through definitions. On the other hand, a report drill-through definition lets you drill through from a source report item to a target report. The target must contain parameters mapped to the correct metadata in the source. This ensures that the target report is filtered correctly. The following figure shows that the target report may be accessed from any studio using the drill-through feature:

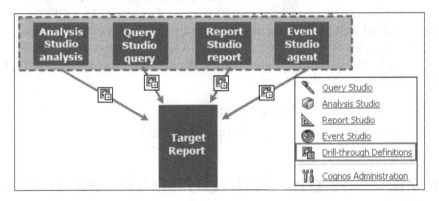

The drill-through access of the source can be defined at the package level via Cognos connection or at the report level while in the Report Studio. In a Cognos package, the scope of data can be controlled, and an option for it is available in the drill-through definition.

The source report does not need to be created when you create the drill-through definition. This will help you set up the drill-through access to the target report, and then you can create as many source reports as you require later. Each package drill-through definition can have only one target report and of course, multiple drill-through definitions can be created for a package.

In a package drill-through definition, you can control where the users can start the drill-through in source reports, and to do this, you have to set a data item in the source package as the scope of the drill-through definition.

If a target report contains one parameter, it makes sense to limit the scope of the drill-through definition to the item, that is, the parameter. This ensures that users will not be prompted to select a parameter value when they drill through. Once you have set the scope of a drill-through definition to a particular data item, users can drill through from a cell in the source report only if its context includes this item.

If you do not set the scope of a drill-through definition for a package, users can drill through from any cell in any report that is created using the package.

Creating a drill-through feature/definition

Depending on the permissions, a user will have the drill-through feature option available from different locations. If the user is running a supported browser, the drill-through feature option will also be available along with launching other Cognos studios. The following screenshot shows the drill-though feature along with other Cognos studio options:

If the **Launch** menu is used to start drill-through options, the user will be able to create drill-through definitions that can be used in multiple reports. We shall, however, create a test drill using the Report Studio. As you may see in the previous screenshot, the Report Studio is also available to launch. Once launched, select a package that you want to use for the data model. Let us create a list report as the new report. Populate the list by dragging and dropping columns from the left package/model. We shall create NE_Name as the drill-through field. This newly created report will be our target report, that is, we shall first open some other report, and we shall drill down to this report from that report.

Once all the required fields have been dragged and dropped into list components of the page, save the report as `Drill-Through-Target-Report`. The following screenshot shows the data model, the selected fields, and the report being saved:

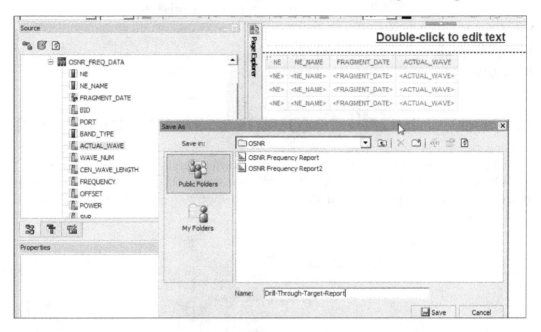

We shall also apply a filter in the target report and send a parameter to this report from the source report. The following screenshot shows that a filter is being applied on the NE_Name field of the target report that is being compared to a parameter value:

Next, we shall open the source report, where we shall set a field that will work as a drill-through field. This means that when we click on that field, it will drill down to the target report that we created and will show the data only for the record that we clicked on in the source report. For doing this, we shall make some changes in the source report. The following screenshot shows the page view of the source report:

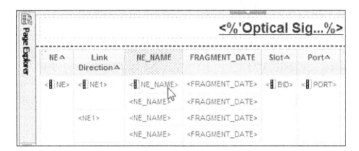

Right-click on the NE_Name column of the source report in the page view and go to the **Drill-Through Definitions 1** option. A dialog will open up, as shown in the following screenshot:

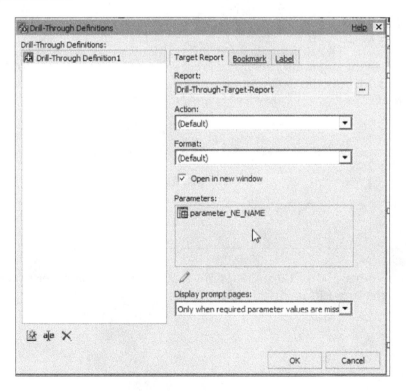

Create a new drill-through report using **Open** on the bottom-left corner of the dialog box. Select the target report that we created earlier in the Report field. You may open a new window when the NE_Name link is clicked on. Also select and configure the parameter for this dialog box. This parameter will be set as a list containing values. Once all the values for the dialog box have been set, click on **ok**. The source report's NE_Name column will change to links.

Now we shall run this report. On running, it may be observed that when we click on any row in the NE_Name column, it opens up a new window where we can see the data only for the record that we selected. The next screenshot shows the source report where the NE_Name column is being shown as a hyperlink pointing to the target report. Once it is clicked on, the target report appears in a new window or tab with only the relevant data.

Link Direction	NE_NAME	Slot	Port	Central Wavelength (nm)	Frequency (Thz)	OSNR
1287 ISB-NOSH	ISB-NOSH	5	1	1,541.35	194.5	22.2
				1,547.7	193.7	20.9
				1,557.37	192.5	19.1
				1,558.17	192.4	19.7

Once the link in the previous screenshot is clicked on, it drills through to the target report with only the data that we want. The following screenshot shows the target report:

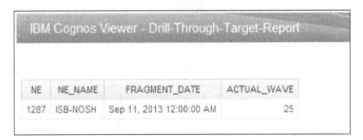

IBM Cognos Viewer - Drill-Through-Target-Report

NE	NE_NAME	FRAGMENT_DATE	ACTUAL_WAVE
1287	ISB-NOSH	Sep 11, 2013 12:00:00 AM	25

There are a number of drill-through options that we may use in order to create a dynamic and feature-full report.

Summary

In this chapter, we covered the drill-through definitions. The drill-through feature provides flexibility to end users while viewing the data.

In the next chapter, we will discuss logging, auditing, performance, and Cognos backups.

7
Logging, Auditing, and Cognos Backups

Administrators are concerned about system availability, stability, speed, security, and troubleshooting. In this chapter, some core administrative tasks will be discussed that help in troubleshooting a problem and enabling Cognos content backups. The following topics will be discussed in this chapter:

- Logging
- Backups

Logging

IBM Cognos BI uses log messages to help administrators diagnose and troubleshoot problems that are faced in the Cognos environment. In other words, it can be used to investigate and diagnose the behavior of the Cognos BI system. Events, errors, warnings, and informative messages are sent to the logging service that redirects the log message data to either a flat file or a remote log server. IBM Cognos BI supports logging to a flat file as well as to a database. Database logging is not just information in the form of log messages, but it includes the mechanism for recording events related to jobs, reports, queries, e-mails, or user logins.

Administrators may determine the logging configuration that is suitable for the environment.

By default, the IBM Cognos BI server is configured to send log messages to a flat file called `cogserver.log`. It is stored in the `logs` folder in the Cognos installation path. There are many other files in this path. Every file present in this path stores messages and logs for different functionalities of applications.

Log messages can provide information about the Cognos configuration, start and stop activities, completion of processing requests, and also act as an indicator of warnings. Audit logs provide information about a user and report activities.

To prepare for logging, there are three major steps involved: the Planning phase, the Configuration phase, and the Setting up Logging Level phase. Each step is briefly discussed as follows:

1. During Planning, the administrator has to determine the logging model that is better for the environment. There are certain logging repositories available in IBM Cognos BI that include flat file (`cogserver.log`), database, `event log` (Windows), `syslog` (Unix, Linux), and remote log servers. The targets for logging must be secure in order to avoid tempering. The following screenshot shows the configuration window and the option where we can add new logging resources. The destination of the new resources can be a file, database, event log, or Linux log.

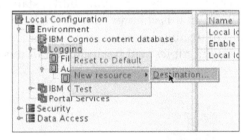

2. While performing a logging configuration, the initial setup for logging is performed, for example, the number of logfiles to be created, the size of each logfile, and the database connection properties. The following screenshot shows the available options for file logging:

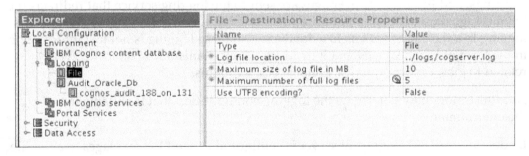

The preceding screenshot is from the IBM Cognos Configuration window. The **File** option is highlighted, and on the right-hand side, all the available options possible for **File** can be seen.

Here's another example of message logging for the purpose of configuring Cognos BI audit logging. The configuration of a database logging in terms of the connection properties is shown in the following screenshot, where the administrator has configured Oracle database logging:

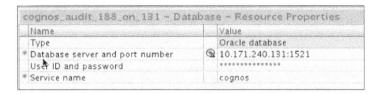

3. Once the database configuration is over, we need to configure the logging levels. Logging levels maintain the amount or details of information saved in the log messages. In the third step, the logging level is configured using the IBM Cognos BI Administration portal. The default minimum level does not capture anything in a database, although basic logs are still captured in the cogserver.log file. The logging level must be carefully selected as it also lowers the system's performance. A basic or report level is recommended. The setting of the logging level is inversely proportional to the system's performance. The lower the logging level, the higher the system performance and vice versa.

The procedure to alter logging levels is as follows:

1. Start IBM Cognos BI Connection, log in, and select **IBM Cognos Administration**.

2. On the **Status** tab, click on **System**, and in the upper-left corner of the **Scorecard** pane, go to **Set properties** of **All dispatchers or services**. The following screenshot shows this scenario:

3. Once the **Set properties** window is open, click on the **Settings** tab, then select **Logging** from the **Category** drop-down menu. Many logging options may be seen here. The level of each task's logging may be set here. The following screenshot shows a few items with their logging levels. This screenshot was taken from a live environment. Note that the default logging level is **Minimal**.

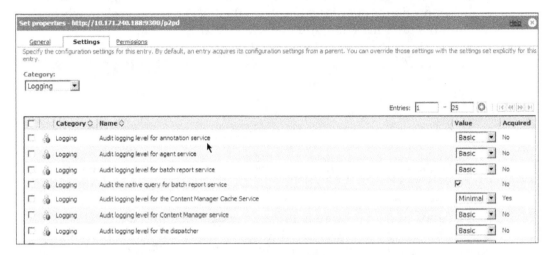

Content auditing

Audit reports may be used for capacity planning, licensing conformance, performance monitoring, and to identify unused Cognos BI contents.
The following procedure will help to configure Cognos Audit Reports:

1. Create a resource as a database in the Cognos Configuration window.
2. Set up the audit level in the database.
3. Enable native query logging.
4. Configure the audit model and audit reports.

The audit model is provided by IBM Cognos BI and is saved in `Audit.cpf` upon navigating through `c10_location/webcontent/samples/models/Audit/`. The sample audit reports are saved in `IBM_Cognos_Audit.zip` upon navigating through `c10_location /webcontent/samples/content/`. A data source connection to the logging database is also required prior to running any of the reports extracted from the samples. The preceding ZIP file needs to be placed in `<install_path>/deployment`, and then may be imported to Cognos. A `Sample` folder containing many reports will be created on successful import. A bundle of reports will be available that may be run as and when required.

Cognos BI takes care of the sensitive information of the user's data model while displaying Cognos error messages on the Cognos Connection. This is done by assigning a unique reference to each error that arises. A sequential number is assigned to an error each day. A very basic error code and a message are displayed to users. However a complete secure error message ID is also displayed along with the timestamp. Cognos administrators may trace down this error to the `cogserver.log` file. For example, the error number in the following message is `secureErrorID:2013-9-20-10:31:15.343-#2`:

An error has occurred. Please contact your administrator. The complete error has been logged by CAF with SecureErrorID: 2013-9-20-10:31:15.343-#2

The Cognos administrator will have to open the `cogserver.log` file using any text editor and search for the error code ID to find the complete error message. Cognos BI also supports user-specific logging.

The procedure is given just after the upcoming table. The following table shows the levels at which various types of information are captured:

Details	Minimal	Basic	Request	Trace	Full
Logging system and services startup, and shutdown and runtime errors	✔	✔	✔	✔	✔
User account logging, runtime usage		✔	✔	✔	✔
User requests	✔	✔		✔	✔
Service requests and responses			✔		✔
Every request to all components including parameter values				✔	✔
Native queries (queries to Cognos components)				✔	✔

Table 1

Backups

To avoid a disaster or to go back in time, we must have the most recent copies of our data that includes the content store (database), configurations (`cogstartup<date/ time-stamp>.xml`), the cryptographic key directories, framework manager projects, images stored in web contents, logfiles, and so on.

Performing regular backups is mandatory, and it is the responsibility of the Cognos administrator to save backups of each of the preceding items in a secure place. The developers also need to have a backup copy of all their projects (packages and reports). This will prevent loss of data. Once a problematic machine is replaced, the data can be easily restored back to the server.

To back up the content store database, the **DBA (Database Administrator)** may schedule the backup depending upon the frequency required. The content store may also be automatically backed up and replicated if there is more than one Content Manager in the environment. Of course one Content Manager will be working as active and the remaining will be functioning as Standby Content Managers.

The `configurations` directory within the Cognos BI installation path is equally important as it saves critical configurations for the whole environment. This directory may be copied and pasted to a location on the same machine as well as on a backup secure storage.

Developers and modelers are required to keep framework manager projects either in source-safe control or in a secure, remote location each time they make changes to the model and packages.

Cognos contents may also be saved in the form of deployment exports. The following procedure explains both exporting and importing contents along with certain important options that are supplied in the deployment wizards.

Let's import one of the built-in samples that Cognos BI provides. The following screenshot shows the path where the samples are located. The `Cognos_Audit_Log.zip` sample will be copied to the `deployment` folder of the Cognos BI environment.

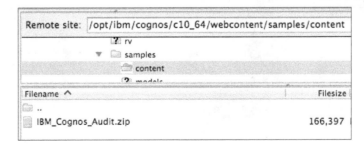

From the preceding path, the `IBM_Cognos_Audit.zip` file needs to be copied and pasted to the `deployment` folder. The following screenshot shows the deployment archive path where we need to place the sample archive:

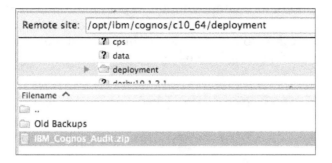

The **Content Administration** section resides under the **Configuration** tab in the Cognos BI Administration portal as shown in the following screenshot. The folders seen in the screenshot are created for convenience and organizing content exports and import archives. This area is blank otherwise. The archive files that were either exported or imported once can be seen in the following screenshot. The icons are different for both types of files. The Cognos audit sample archive will not be visible here unless we import it once.

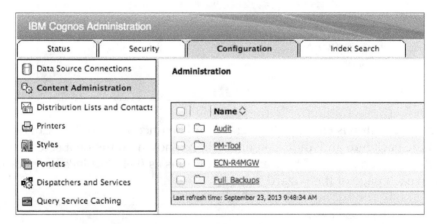

Content management and backups – importing

There are several options, for example, import, export, index, maintenance, and so on. We will only focus on the import and export functionalities that are relevant to this chapter title. There is a toolbar in the top-right corner of the content management screen, as shown in the following screenshot. Click on the **New Import** option.

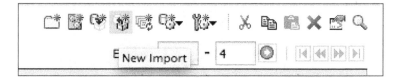

The preceding audit archive will become viewable and selectable as shown in the following screenshot. Select it and click on **Next**.

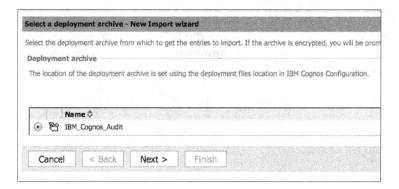

Once the **Next** button is clicked, the archive will be uncompressed by Cognos BI Server at the backend, and all its contents will be shown on the next screen as shown in the following screenshot. There are other options as well, but let's keep the default options on each page of the wizard.

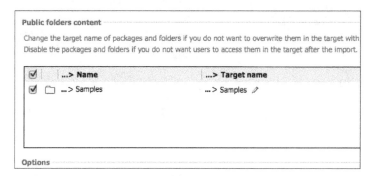

On the last page of the wizard, also viewable in the following figure, there is an option to upgrade the report specifications. This may be selected if we are importing an archive that was created in an older version of Cognos, for example, prior to Version 10.2.

Report specification upgrade:
You may want to keep existing report specification versions for compatibility with existing applications.

○ Upgrade all report specifications to the latest version
● Keep the existing report specification versions

Once the job has been started, it takes some time depending upon the size as well as the nature of the contents included in the archive file that needs to be imported. Roughly, this time is less than a minute. The following screenshot provides a summary of the import process once it is completed. The warnings, failures, information, time, status, and certain other flags are displayed on this screen.

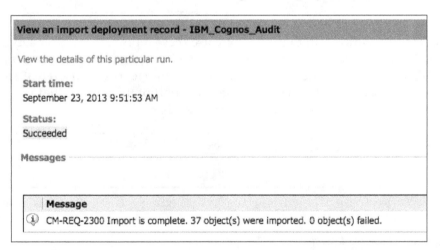

The contents have been imported under **Public Folders** (as shown in the following screenshot) with the name **Samples**. The directory administrators may specify permissions to only relevant users once the import process has been completed.

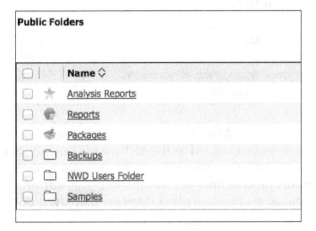

End users (administrators in this case) may use these reports to monitor servers and user sessions, and these reports will also help in capacity and license planning for the Cognos BI Server' environment. A few of the contents (reports and events) are visible in the following screenshot. These contents were part of the archive that we just imported. There are two events and six reports.

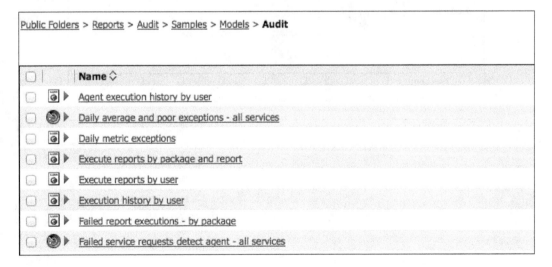

Content management and backups – exporting

The Cognos Content Management section in the Administration portal is a key feature and is used to back up content as well as to deploy contents from the development to the production environment. This job may also be scheduled to dump a selected or complete content store backup on a defined frequency. The **New Export** option is visible in the following screenshot:

On selecting the **New Export** option, a wizard similar to the Import Wizard starts asking for information. All the screens and options are self-explanatory as the description is written for each option. Let's rename the export process as **Test Import** and the description may be specified. The following screenshot gives a snapshot of the first step of the export wizard:

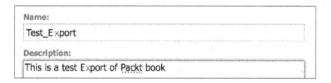

The next step is to select the method of deployment. The Export wizard gives a default option to select the public folders and directory contents manually. It also gives the option to export the entire content store either with the user account information or without it. This second option is useful for taking either a backup of the entire content or when shifting from one server to another server as it also carries the user's account information. In the first option, the administrator needs to explicitly select the content that needs to be exported. The following screenshot shows both the options for deployment method as well as their nested options:

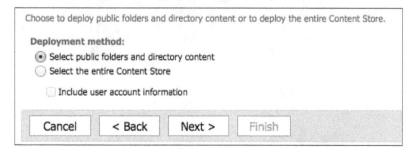

Selecting the **Select the entire Content Store** option including user account information is a useful way to back up the content store, so it can easily be restored later on if required. The wizard is quite flexible for selecting content multiple times. Folders and package folders are the two content types that can be selected. This means the content that needs to be exported must be enclosed in a folder. All content, subfolders, and their contents are automatically selected. The following screenshot shows the content selection page where the **Samples** folder has been selected:

In the following screenshot, the wizard is asking if this deployment job needs to be run immediately or at a specific time. This option is imported because if the deployment job contains too much content, it will degrade system performance if run during working hours.

Finally, when the **Run** button is clicked on in the preceding step, Cognos starts to export all the specified content to a deployment archive, that is a compressed file. After the completion of the process, the deployment wizard shows the summary of the process with all the details of the process status, completion time, and so on. The following screenshot shows the summary of the export process. The ZIP archive is placed at `<Cognos_install_path>/deployment folder`.

Summary

After completing this chapter, readers should be able to work on logging, taking backups of contents, and moving contents between servers.

In the next chapter, we will discuss some additional configurations and customizations.

8
Additional Configurations and Customization

When it comes to user experience, the graphical user interface plays a major role in bringing about a good user experience. Since the very start of Cognos BI, the Cognos BI application developers focused on attaining a much better user experience by providing some excellent and advanced features. These features not only help in quick content management, but also provide a very user-friendly environment. In this chapter we will introduce the additional features that Cognos has along with the customization of the Cognos environment. The following topics will be covered in this chapter:

- Customizing appearance
- Customizing functionality
- Portlets administration
- Managing user profiles

Customizing the appearance

Cognos provides a professional web interface where all the studios are web-based. This includes Query Studio, Report Studio, Event Studio, Analysis Studio, Cognos Workspace, Cognos Workspace Advanced, and much more. Of course, there is Cognos Connection as well as Cognos Administration Portal. The Cognos BI environment provides flexibility and adaptability to change almost all the appearance sections of the studios and connections, as per the requirements of different organizations. For example, a company would always want the company logo next to each professional business report. A company has a color scheme, font styles, sizes, images, and a logo that apply to the company's official website, internal portals, and even the company letter heads and employee visiting cards.

IBM Cognos BI provides some built-in styles (CSS, skins). Once applied globally by an administrator, it changes the global look and feel of almost all the sections (studios, connections, Admin Portal). The IBM Cognos BI administrator may change the default style by altering the **Styles** section of the default user preferences from the Cognos namespace residing in the **Security** tab. Cognos BI also provides the flexibility to add custom styles (containing custom colors, fonts, images, and so on). The following screenshot shows some of the different predefined styles available:

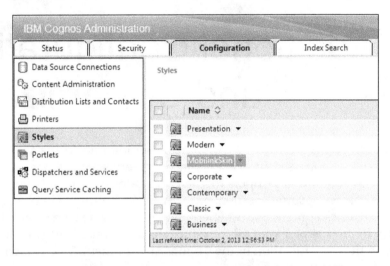

Styles may also be changed from the style management utility, which is located on each Cognos BI Gateway. A custom style may be created by duplicating the existing style and editing it. When a user logs in for the first time, a default style is tagged for this user and is hardcoded, unless the user manually changes it. If you disable all styles except the preferred style, the user cannot change the style as there is only one style available. Therefore, the administrator must apply the company style prior to allowing access to users. Otherwise, it will be very difficult to change the style company wide. When no other style is available, Cognos BI uses the **Corporate** style. The following screenshot shows the Cognos namespace's default Cognos user preferences section with the company style selected as default for all new users:

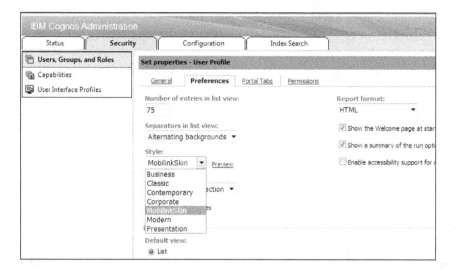

A detailed procedure for customizing the Cognos styles is available on the Cognos website, where every section is discussed separately.

The following link points to the IBM Cognos BI 10.2 documentation homepage:

`http://pic.dhe.ibm.com/infocenter/cbi/v10r2m0/index.jsp`

Try searching for *Customizing the Appearance of Cognos*.

Creating a custom style manually

The following steps briefly explain how a custom Cognos style can be created:

1. Select an existing style that best suits your choice. The style management utility may be used for this purpose. Rename this style, for example, the company name along with the directory location in the skins directory.

2. Custom fonts, CSS, images, and layout properties may be included. Refer to the file located at `c10_location/webcontent/skins/style`. The CSS file usually contains the details of fonts, colors, and so on. Also, a lot of the changes are made using XML.

3. In IBM Cognos Administration Portal, under the **Configurations** tab, create a new style item and provide the relative path to the directory created earlier.

4. Once a style has been created, it can be used as a default user style by selecting it in the **Default User Preferences** settings. These settings are located under the **Security** tab in the Cognos namespace.

The style management utility

Cognos BI also provides a command-line-based utility to manage styles. The gateway servers contain this utility that is located at the Cognos installation path. Once the styles are created, they can be used as the basis for creating other custom styles. Once the custom styles are created using this utility, XML files may be used to make global customizations to the appearance of the Cognos Connection and Administration portals. XML validation is also performed by this utility. Once these files are created, they are saved to **Content Manager**. Once published, these styles are visible to users. The following steps show you how to create and deploy a custom style using this utility for Cognos Administration:

1. **Create a custom style**: You can create a custom style that is based on one of the predefined styles provided by IBM Cognos BI.

2. **Modify the style.xml file**: When you create a new style, changes to Cognos Connection and Cognos Administration can be made via the `style.xml` file located at `c10_location/temp`.

3. **Generate the custom style**: The utility creates a temporary folder at `c10_location/temp` for the new style. This folder contains the files necessary for the new style, including CSS and images. For the IBM Cognos Connection and Administration portals, the style changes are updated dynamically by the utility. Fonts and layout properties can be changed by manually changing the `.css` files.

4. **Deploy the style**: To deploy a style, create a folder and move all the `.css`, images, and `.xml` files to your desired style name folder and move this folder to `c10_location\webcontent\skins` on all the gateway locations.

5. **Publish the custom style**: By performing this step, the style becomes available to all users to use and appears in the list of styles in IBM Cognos Connection. This is done by the administrator adding the style from Cognos Administration Portal. The name and relative path to the style folder are provided.

Customizing the functionalities

Certain functionalities of the IBM Cognos BI environment can also be changed and customized as per your requirements. You must be careful to move the changes done in the system.xml files in some previous versions of Cognos. The following areas can be focused on while customizing Cognos functionalities:

- Customizing IBM Cognos Connection
- Customizing the login page
- Changing the default Query Studio template
- Customizing server-side printing
- Enabling the Query Studio to start in the safe mode
- Customizing date formats
- Customizing the CSV output format properties
- Customizing the auto-size feature for search and select prompts
- Customizing Batch Report Service and report services
- Customizing error handling for the SMTP mail server
- Disabling the Report E-mail Attachments feature
- Customizing scheduling
- Changing default file extensions for Excel 2002 spreadsheets
- Customizing the printing styles for Excel 2007 reports
- Disabling or enabling the **Web Page**, **RSS Feed**, **Image**, **Text**, and **My Inbox** features.

A detailed description is available on the Cognos BI 10.2 documentation website by searching for *Customizing the functionality of IBM Cognos software* on the link provided at the end of the *Customizing the appearance* section.

Administration of Portlets

The IBM Cognos portal services provide a collection of small portlets that maybe used in other IBM Cognos BI sections, for example, Cognos Connection and even in other portals. Cognos BI has many portlets that are divided into four major sections. These sections further provide different portlets, which are as follows:

- IBM Cognos Utility
  - Bookmarks Viewer
  - Image Viewer
  - RSS Viewer
  - HTML Source
  - HTML Viewer

- **Dashboard | Multi-page**
  - IBM Cognos Content
  - IBM Cognos Navigator
  - IBM Cognos Search
  - IBM Cognos Viewer

- IBM Cognos Extended Applications

Furthermore, new portlets can be created, which may contain either one or multiple portlets from the preceding list. The following screenshot shows a view of the available options for portlets. A customized portlet named **ECN-PS-Core** is a created. This customized portlet can be used in Cognos Connection, for example, while creating a new tab page.

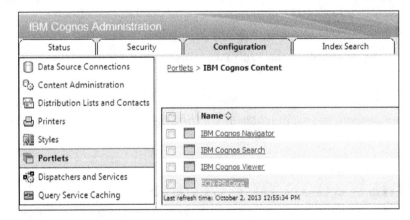

Managing user profiles

User profiles contain the **Portal** tab and personal folder contents. They also have user preferences such as language, preferred output format, the style used, and the Cognos Connections view settings. The default user profile applies to all new users, and this profile is created when a user logs in for the first time. The directory administrators can edit the default user profile for all users from the Cognos namespace settings. The administrator can also copy one profile's settings to another profile from the **Security** tab. This function is located under the **Security** tab as the third option.

Summary

This chapter briefly introduced readers to customizations that can be performed in the IBM Cognos BI environment. After the completion of this chapter, the Cognos portals can be customized as per the organization's requirements.

In the next chapter we will discuss the administration of new and enhanced features.

9
Administration of New and Enhanced Features

Surely, readers are more concerned about the new features of the new version and their administration. By now, we have briefly covered a major portion of the administration. We will now cover few more areas that have been developed in Version 10.1 and onwards. Major topics to be covered in this chapter are:

- Cognos Mobile
- Multiple-tenant environments

Cognos Mobile

IBM Cognos Mobile is a new feature introduced in Cognos BI Version 10.1. Cognos Mobile carries features to view reports directly on smartphones and tablets. These reports may include reports authored by Query Studio, Report Studio, or Analysis Studio. These reports can be downloaded. To make Cognos Mobile work, several components are needed on the IBM Cognos BI server, and users accessing Cognos reports on mobile device require a native client on the smartphone.

Cognos Mobile supports in displaying content-rich reports on mobile handsets. It also supports the Cognos BI prompt functionality and scheduling. In case of loss of mobile, Cognos BI Administrator now has the capability to remotely remove sensitive contents from the device. There is, however, a restriction to install the same version of Cognos both for Mobile and BI server.

New features for Cognos Mobile in Version 10.2

The new features for Cognos Mobile in Version 10.2 are as follows:

- Push notifications for iOS (Apple) devices
- An access-restriction feature — security can be applied to users working from Cognos Mobile
- Burst reporting
- Support for new languages

Cognos Mobile components

Cognos Mobile setup requires an installation of the **Cognos Mobile service** where the application tier and gateway reside. The second component is at the client end, and it is the **Cognos Mobile client**. For devices such as Blackberry, Cognos Mobile also needs to communicate to the **BB Enterprise Server** and **MDS Connection Service** components. The following diagram briefly shows the components interacting in an environment:

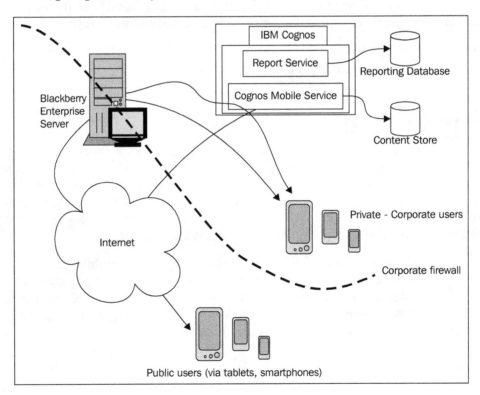

Cognos Mobile service

A few responsibilities of Cognos Mobile service are as follows:

- To keep both BI servers' mobile content store synced with mobile database on mobile device
- To transfer contents (such as reports) to mobile devices after compressing them (for fast transfer)
- To convert the Cognos BI contents (such as, reports, analyses) to the format supported for rendering contents on mobile device
- To communicate with mobile devices and exchange requests between the BI server and mobile devices
- To convert **Cognos BI SOAP (Cognos Business Intelligence Simple Object Access Protocol)** format messages to wireless-friendly messages

Cognos Mobile rich client

Cognos Mobile works on the phenomenon of client-server architecture. To interact with IBM Cognos BI Server via Cognos Gateway, the mobile handset must have a rich client application (in the case of Blackberry handsets) that can exchange data between the server and handset. A mobile device has a mobile rich client as well as a compact, compressed content store that also supports content encryption. This client application has all the required capabilities to interact with the BI server. In the case of other smartphones (such as iOS devices), there is a separate application.

RIM (Research In Motion) owns Blackberry smartphones. It also has Enterprise Server that supports and manages security, contents, devices, and data flows. This Enterprise Server is managed by organizations themselves, and it is internal to the organization. Cognos BI uses BlackBerry MDS Connection Service to support Cognos Mobile on Blackberry handsets.

The following screenshot shows how Cognos reports appear on a mobile device:

Installing and configuring Cognos Mobile

Let's briefly discuss the installation and configuration steps for Cognos Mobile:

1. Check the existing Cognos BI environment and review it first.

2. Download the Cognos Mobile pack from the IBM Cognos BI resources.

3. For installing Cognos Mobile to the same path where other components of Cognos BI are already installed, Cognos service needs to be stopped first.

4. Start the Cognos setup (`./issetup` for Unix flavors and `issetup.exe` for Windows).

5. The installation wizard is pretty straightforward. Follow the instructions during setup.

6. After the setup is finished, start the IBM Cognos configuration (`./cogconfig.sh` for Linux and navigate to **Start | IBM Cognos 10 | configuration** for Windows).

7. Configure Blackberry MDS Connection Service. (The complete procedure is mentioned in the installation manual for Cognos Mobile.)

8. Configure the Mobile content store just in case **Content Manager** is not on this server. Once we start the Cognos service, Cognos Mobile related tables will be automatically created in the content store.

9. Save the configuration and start the Cognos service.

10. For setting up the database client to connect the Cognos Mobile service to content store. The connectivity is established using **JDBC (Java Database Connectivity)** drivers that are installed with Cognos BI.

11. Cognos Mobile can use the same content store that Cognos BI is using, or it can also use some other database. Settings for every RDBMS are almost different, and in some cases, paid drivers are needed to establish connectivity (such as Microsoft SQL Server).

12. To check if Cognos Mobile is working properly, click on **Environment** from the **Explorer** window of **IBM Cognos Configuration**. If the Mobile service that is enabled is visible and its value is set to **true** in the properties of the IBM Cognos BI service, this means that the installation was successful and it is working.

IBM Cognos BI Version 10.2 now has a separate capability to manage the Cognos Mobile security.

The users can now be restricted to use Cognos Mobile if required. Running a report on Cognos Mobile is pretty easy, and since the user interface is very simple, users may navigate to a particular report and run it in the same fashion as it is run in the IBM Cognos Connection on a desktop.

Multiple-tenant environments

A multiple-tenant environment is another new feature of Cognos BI Version 10.2 has.

After the introduction of cloud computing, one cloud service provider had to deal with multiple customers or organizations at a time. A feature was also added in Cognos to support multiple customers or organizations on the same (single) deployment.

By using the multiple-tenant feature for Cognos, organizations can only see their own data. Data for other organizations running on the same deployment is invisible to each of the other organizations. This is an efficient use of resources and money. Existing authentication providers can be used to manage users and groups, resulting in no additional administration tasks. Cognos also supports sharing of content between two tenants (organizations or customers) by declaring them public and setting suitable access and tenancy permissions.

To configure multi-tenancy, there are two steps:

* Identifying tenancy information
* Turning multi-tenancy on or off

Identifying tenancy information

The IBM Cognos configuration needs to be modified before using the Cognos multi-tenancy feature. The following methods can help identify tenancy information:

- Using hierarchies
- Using object properties
- Using custom code (when the first two methods fail)

Turning multi-tenancy on or off

Setting advanced authentication properties on all **Content Manager** servers enables multi-tenancy and removing all advanced authentication properties disables it.

Tenant administration

Since multiple tenants can be stored in the same content store, a tenant ID is associated with each object that is created. Cognos system administrators have full access to tenant information. Tenant-related administrative tasks are performed by Cognos system administrators. This is done from the IBM Cognos BI Configuration window.

Summary

This chapter covered Cognos Mobile and multi-tenancy, two of the key new features of IBM Cognos BI Version 10.2.

Index

Thank you for buying
IBM Cognos BI v10.2
Administration Essentials

About Packt Publishing

Packt, pronounced 'packed', published its first book "Mastering phpMyAdmin for Effective MySQL Management" in April 2004 and subsequently continued to specialize in publishing highly focused books on specific technologies and solutions.

Our books and publications share the experiences of your fellow IT professionals in adapting and customizing today's systems, applications, and frameworks. Our solution based books give you the knowledge and power to customize the software and technologies you're using to get the job done. Packt books are more specific and less general than the IT books you have seen in the past. Our unique business model allows us to bring you more focused information, giving you more of what you need to know, and less of what you don't.

Packt is a modern, yet unique publishing company, which focuses on producing quality, cutting-edge books for communities of developers, administrators, and newbies alike. For more information, please visit our website: www.packtpub.com.

About Packt Enterprise

In 2010, Packt launched two new brands, Packt Enterprise and Packt Open Source, in order to continue its focus on specialization. This book is part of the Packt Enterprise brand, home to books published on enterprise software – software created by major vendors, including (but not limited to) IBM, Microsoft and Oracle, often for use in other corporations. Its titles will offer information relevant to a range of users of this software, including administrators, developers, architects, and end users.

Writing for Packt

We welcome all inquiries from people who are interested in authoring. Book proposals should be sent to author@packtpub.com. If your book idea is still at an early stage and you would like to discuss it first before writing a formal book proposal, contact us; one of our commissioning editors will get in touch with you.

We're not just looking for published authors; if you have strong technical skills but no writing experience, our experienced editors can help you develop a writing career, or simply get some additional reward for your expertise.

IBM Cognos Business Intelligence

IBM Cognos Business Intelligence

ISBN: 978-1-84968-356-2   Paperback: 318 pages

Discover the practical approach to BI with IBM Cognos Business Intelligence

1. Learn how to better administer your IBM Cognos 10 environment in order to improve productivity and efficiency

2. Empower your business with the latest Business Intelligence (BI) tools

3. Discover advanced tools and knowledge that can greatly improve daily tasks and analysis

IBM Cognos Business Intelligence 10.1 Dashboarding Cookbook

ISBN: 978-1-84968-582-5   Paperback: 206 pages

Working with dashboards in IBM Cognos BI 10.1: Design, distribute, and collaborate

1. Exploring and interacting with IBM Cognos Business Insight and Business Insight Advanced

2. Creating dashboards in IBM Cognos Business Insight and Business Insight Advanced

3. Sharing and collaborating on dashboards using portlets

Please check **www.PacktPub.com** for information on our titles

IBM Cognos TM1 Developer's Certification Guide

Fast track your way to COG-310 certification!

James D. Miller

IBM Cognos TM1 Developer's Certification guide

ISBN: 978-1-84968-490-3   Paperback: 240 pages

Fast track your way to COG-310 certification!

1. Successfully clear COG-310 certification

2. Master the major components that make up Cognos TM1 and learn the function of each

3. Understand the advantages of using Rules versus Turbo Integrator

IBM Cognos Insight

Take a deep dive into IBM Cognos Insight and learn how this personal analytics tool can be integrated with other IBM Business Analytics products

Sanjeev Datta

IBM Cognos Insight

ISBN: 978-1-84968-846-8   Paperback: 142 pages

Take a deep dive into IBM Cognos Insight and learn how this personal analytics tool can be integrated with other IBM Business Analytics products

1. Step-by-step, how to guide, for installing and configuring IBM Cognos Insight for your needs

2. Learn how to build financial, marketing, and sales workspaces in Cognos Insight

3. Learn how to integrate and collaborate with IBM Cognos Business Intelligence

Please check **www.PacktPub.com** for information on our titles

www.ingramcontent.com/pod-product-compliance
Lightning Source LLC
Chambersburg PA
CBHW060154060326
40690CB00018B/4102